motown in love

edited and with an introduction by **herb jordan**

motown in love

lyrics from the golden era

pantheon books, new york

Library of Congress Cataloging-in-Publication Data
Motown in love : lyrics from the golden era / edited and with an introduction
by Herb Jordan.
   p. cm.
  ISBN 0-375-42200-5
  1. Soul music — Texts.   2. Love songs — Texts.   3. Popular music — 1961–1970 — Texts.
I. Jordan, Herb.
ML54.6.M675 2006
782.421644'0268 — dc22   2006045149

www.pantheonbooks.com

Book design by Iris Weinstein

Printed in the United States of America

First Edition

9 8 7 6 5 4 3 2 1

To my parents James and Ilene Jordan,
for six decades of devotion.

The minute I heard my first love story, I started looking for you, not knowing how blind that was. Lovers don't finally meet somewhere. They're in each other all along.

Rumi

contents

half a mile from heaven: the love songs of motown   *xv*

lessons of love

all in love is fair   *2*
ask the lonely   *3*
back in my arms again   *4*
beauty is only skin deep   *6*
does your mama know about me   *8*
don't look back   *10*
the hunter gets captured by the game   *11*
if it's magic   *12*
i'll be doggone   *13*
it takes two   *14*
the love i saw in you was just a mirage   *15*
the love you save   *16*
shop around   *18*
uptight (everything's all right)   *20*
you beat me to the punch   *21*
you can't hurry love   *23*
when i'm gone   *25*

the path to your heart

do you love me   *28*
get ready   *30*
he was really sayin' somthin'   *32*
hitch hike   *33*

i'll try something new   34

i'm gonna make you love me   35

it's growing   37

stubborn kind of fellow   38

when the lovelight starts shining through his eyes   39

the promise

baby i'm for real   42

if this world were mine   43

i'll be there   44

reach out i'll be there   45

you're all i need to get by   46

the joy of love

ain't no mountain high enough   48

ain't nothing like the real thing   50

as   51

dancing in the street   55

for once in my life   57

how sweet it is to be loved by you   58

if i could build my whole world around you   59

loving you is sweeter than ever   60

the one who really loves you   61

pride and joy   62

signed, sealed, delivered, i'm yours   63

up the ladder to the roof   65

the way you do the things you do   67

you are the sunshine of my life   68

you're a wonderful one   69

your precious love   71

when a man loves a woman

bernadette 74

i can't get next to you 76

i can't help myself 78

i second that emotion 80

i was made to love her 81

let's get it on 83

more love 85

my cherie amour 86

my girl 87

my girl has gone 88

never can say goodbye 90

this old heart of mine 92

too busy thinking about my baby 94

you're my everything 95

the love of a woman

baby love 98

come see about me 100

don't mess with bill 102

i hear a symphony 104

if i were your woman 106

my guy 108

please mr. postman 109

stop! in the name of love 111

under your spell

baby i need your loving 114

distant lover 116

every little bit hurts 117

heat wave   118

i'll be in trouble   120

love is like an itching in my heart   121

nowhere to run   123

standing in the shadows of love   125

until you come back to me (that's what i'm gonna do)   127

you keep me hangin' on   128

you've really got a hold on me   130

love is strange

ain't that peculiar   134

choosey beggar   136

devil with the blue dress   137

just my imagination (running away with me)   138

love is here and now you're gone   140

truly yours   142

two lovers   143

love lost

come and get these memories   146

fading away   147

i heard it through the grapevine   148

(i know) i'm losing you   150

never dreamed you'd leave in summer   151

i want you back   152

i wish it would rain   154

it's the same old song   155

lately   157

my world is empty without you   158

ooo baby baby   160

reflections   161

rocket love   163

7 rooms of gloom   165

shake me, wake me (when it's over)   166

since i lost my baby   168

take me in your arms (rock me)   170

the tears of a clown   171

the tracks of my tears   173

what becomes of the brokenhearted   175

where did our love go   177

who's lovin' you   179

yester-me, yester-you, yesterday   180

higher love

love's in need of love today   182

what's going on   183

acknowledgments   185

a note on the lyrics   186

permissions acknowledgments   187

half a mile from heaven: the love songs of motown

D etroit in the 1960s was an unlikely stage for a production that featured some of the most inspirational love songs ever written. It may seem equally unlikely that most of those songs were written by young black men. Default notions of romance are an awkward overlay to the reality of this city of steel and sweat, Joe Louis and Jimmy Hoffa. Rough? Tanks that rolled off Detroit's assembly lines and onto Europe's beaches as liberators returned home twenty years later to quell urban rebellion. But there was no simple way to quiet the musical movement that was surging in the basements and on the street corners of Detroit's black neighborhoods.

The city vibrated. Every block had a band, it seemed, and on summer nights young men harmonized under the streetlights. Mixed in with homegrown versions of hits by Ben E. King and the Moonglows were original songs penned by the neighborhood tunesmith. Sunday morning you had to arrive early to get a seat at church. Overcome with the spirit, preachers resorted to singing their sermons. At New Bethel Baptist Church you didn't mind standing for two hours if you could hear the Franklin sisters—Aretha, Carolyn, and Erma—sing "How I Got Over."

But there was a new sound. As word spread through the neighborhood, teenagers scrambled, high-top shoes and bicycles, to the parking lot of the Bi-Lo Supermarket where on a makeshift stage twelve-year-old Stevie Wonder performed "Fingertips." Before long, record store clerks were inundated with customers describing, and sometimes attempting to sing, a few bars of the sound they heard on their transistor radios.

These were the 1960s, and poverty, segregation, Vietnam, and nuclear gamesmanship convened in a funnel cloud that threatened to rip through the American fabric. But with the innocence of a first kiss, the poets of Motown conjured up a black Camelot and took America "up the ladder to the roof" for a view of heaven. From rooftops to blue-lit basements they danced, black and white, fast and slow, as young men testified that they would "find that girl if [they] had to hitch hike 'round the world," and women replied, "ain't no mountain high enough to keep me from getting to you." Boys in the 'hood—long typecast as the least productive, most destructive element of society—wrote knowingly and elegantly of life and love. The young women dazzled with a mix of soul and social graces, grace they maintained even when on Southern highways gunshots were directed at the Motown tour bus.

The thought of white teenagers falling under the spell of black music mobilized the guardians of white culture. Everyone knew the invisible perimeter that insulated white America would soon be irreparably breached. The usual operatives took measures to thwart it. Music was on the front lines of the battle. In retrospect, the last-gasp efforts at interdiction seem comical. A now infamous poster that circulated throughout the South warned white parents not to allow their children to listen to Negro music, lest they end up with *one* on the dance floor or otherwise.

As great as Motown's records were, the company's executives knew the power of live performance. The Motown Revue featured almost the entire roster of artists and a live stage band. The artists were confronted for the first time with overt segregation when the caravan rolled into Southern towns. Neighborhoods in Detroit were neatly divided along racial lines, but in the South the lines were often drawn with firearms. What was taken for granted in Northern cities could be a perilous undertaking in the South. Bobby Rogers of the Miracles recalls that a gas station owner confronted him with a gun after he used a white restroom. White and black teenagers were typically assigned to opposite sides of auditoriums in Southern venues. But on many occasions the police were powerless to enforce the separation as the teenagers, in their own version of a freedom march, just stepped to the beat.

In the mid-1950s television sponsors squirmed at the thought of having their products associated with Nat "King" Cole's variety show; in the absence of commercial support, the show quickly vanished from the air. But by the early 1960s, families gathered on Sunday evenings to watch Ed Sullivan introduce the latest Motown sensation. Disc jockeys thought nothing of sandwiching a Rolling Stones track between hits by Martha and the Vandellas and the Four Tops. The seeds of this social revolution were scattered on the winds of radio and television airwaves. While activists preached and lawyers agitated, Motown crept into white homes, Southern and suburban, through Radio Free America. Once the Marvin Gaye poster went up, there was no turning back. White girls swooned over Marvin as had their mothers for Frank Sinatra. Even in the heartland, white boys earnestly attempted Motown dance routines and, for a moment, imagined that they were black.

The specter that this music might incite race mixing was rivaled only by the fear of images of *black* romance. The myth ran deep that among blacks love was characterized more by physical urges than by the complex universe of emotion that transcends motor response. Thomas Jefferson could have been a Hollywood studio executive when he dismissed sentiment among blacks as "less felt and sooner forgotten." If you didn't see *Porgy and Bess, Carmen Jones,* or *Paris Blues,* you might have missed Hollywood's entire pre-Motown output of film portrayals of black romance. In the age before videotape, DVDs, and cable, most people, black and white, had never seen affection expressed between blacks in film or on television. While major studios ignored black love affairs, the Motown songwriters understood the poetry of Everyman. These songs explored romance's jagged landscape — infatuation, discovery, love's grip, love lost. They told of brokenhearted men and wrote of women who know "how sweet it is."

A sign over the door of the house on Detroit's West Grand Boulevard read Hitsville USA, a slick slogan worthy of the other major presence a half mile down the boulevard, General Motors. Motown's eagerness to market its own assembly line obscured for some what really went on inside that house. Close observers watched the parade of odd-shaped instrument cases that concealed everything from bongos to bassoons and the procession of young men with skinny ties, cropped hair, and satchels stuffed with staff paper. They were the ones who knew the secret language of song. It *was* a production line but one that dispensed magic. Names such as Ivy Jo Hunter, Sylvia Moy, Hank Cosby, and Clarence Paul were scarcely noticed by a public in love with the flourish of sequined stars. The songwriters, invisible architects of the Motown sound, assembled the substance of everyday into songs that were at once sophisticated and earthy, personal and universal. In many ways, it was the Great American Songbook of the second half of the century.

Fans may have believed that Diana Ross wrote "You Can't Hurry Love." She *was* convincing. The truth is, before a song reached the artist a songwriter or two had labored over the turn of a phrase, reshaping it until its internal rhythm and contours fit the music like counterpoint. Not long after the spark of an idea had blossomed into a song, it was thrust into the glare of the Hitsville proving ground. Each song had to run the gauntlet of rival songwriters, producers, and the man who started it all: Mr. Gordy, who himself had written a string of hits. Berry Gordy instinctively knew that great music is built from the song up. Songs were placed on trial and any facet, from the euphonics of the words to chord structure, was fair game. Morris Broadnax who, with a teenage Stevie Wonder and Clarence Paul, wrote the masterwork "Until You Come Back to Me," recalls that "new songs were worked on between Tuesday and Thursday, and on Friday all the songwriters presented their best material to the staff. There was so much great music that you hoped that yours was one of the few chosen on Monday." Collaboration and competition sharpened the writing. Smokey Robinson, Holland-Dozier-Holland, Ashford and Simpson, Strong and Whitfield, and Stevie Wonder would arrive on Fridays and place their latest in the hands of musicians James Jamerson, Benny Benjamin, Robert White, and Earl Van Dyke—the Funk Brothers. Cutting sessions—jazz musicians' venerable device for raising the creative bar—found a home in the basement of Hitsville. It was hand-to-hand musical combat and whoever was left standing made a record.

Love has long been a staple in the American song tradition. Black songwriters have always created the template for jazz and blues, and

W. C. Handy and Duke Ellington knew their way around a love song. But beginning in the 1930s, black artists often looked to Jewish songwriters for a seemingly endless string of pop hits. Cole Porter, Irving Berlin, and George and Ira Gershwin lined the pages of the American songbook with interpretations by the great black singers. The combination was potent. Imagine American song in the absence of Ella Fitzgerald and Louis Armstrong's "Cheek to Cheek" duet or Sarah Vaughan's "April in Paris." This brilliant symbiosis continued in the late '50s and early '60s as black popular artists turned to writers such as Jerry Leiber and Mike Stoller, and Carole King and Gerry Goffin for songs like "Stand by Me" and "Will You Love Me Tomorrow." But Motown—from the musicians and singers to the producers and songwriters—was a community project. While everyone was invited to the party, this music was a product of the tough public housing projects and Detroit's strong black middle-class neighborhoods of neatly cropped lawns, family dinners, and traditions that went back generations. The accumulated musical knowledge of neighborhood masters was summoned. The call went out to poets, arrangers, practitioners of jazz and gospel, and the classically trained to form what writer and producer Clay McMurray describes as a Noah's Ark of talent. The studio was said to have been open twenty-four hours a day, seven days a week.

In the 1960s the times they were a-changin'. Songwriters drew their inspiration from issues of the day. Artists believed in the power of music, that they could change the world with a song. The '60s manifesto assured us that "Blowin' in the Wind" and "We Shall Overcome" could end the war and make the walls of segregation "come tumblin' down." Singer-songwriters chronicled the unfolding social drama, and when they spoke of love it was in the most personal way. Detached, formulaic love songs now seemed anemic, as Bob Dylan and the Beatles redefined the subject matter of popular music. For a love song to grab hold of this generation something different was required.

The Motown writers responded with songs that transformed the prosaic into the poetic. The girl down the block became a goddess, and the path to her heart, an epic journey. From "Bernadette":

And when I speak of you, I see envy in other men's eyes,
and I'm well aware of what's on their minds.
They pretend to be my friend, when all the time
They long to persuade you from my side.
They'd give the world and all they own
For just one moment we have known.

The Motown roster of artists was packed with female vocalists. Men wrote for Mary Wells, the Supremes, the Marvelettes, Martha and the Vandellas, and every other woman on the label. Sylvia Moy's early compositions—"I Was Made to Love Her," "It Takes Two," "My Cherie Amour"—did much to establish a standard of idealized romance. To write effectively for female vocalists, the male songwriters were forced to immerse themselves in a woman's point of view. Women wait for, agonize over, and celebrate love when it finally arrives. The male songwriters rejected Pavlovian swagger; like Marco Polo bearing gifts from a strange land, they delivered to the male vocalists the textures of romance. Gone was the supposed indifference to the joy and pain of love. These writers discovered love as a force of nature, a celestial presence around which pride, reputation, and the grab bag of male defense mechanisms simply orbited. But this was no weak, victim-of-love routine. The men sang songs infused with unmistakable ardor and palpable virility and with the sort of strength that flows from the yin and yang of love. "Ain't Too Proud to Beg" laments, "I know you want to leave me," and then stiffens, "but I *refuse* to let you go." Marvin implored, "Let's get it on," but assured "I won't push you, baby." When the men expressed overblown confidence, it was as a foil for the failure to win the love of a woman. "Can't Get Next to You": "I can live forever if I so desire . . . I can make the grayest sky blue . . . But I can't get next to you."

These were strong men who understood the power of love and women's power in love. Grown men dropped to their knees on stage and wished it would rain. It was this willingness to pierce the façade of male invulnerability that endeared Motown to anyone who had a heart. Smokey: "So, take a good look at my face. / You'll see my smile looks out of place. / If you look closer, it's easy to trace / The tracks of my tears." When it happened, love was strong, supportive, and reciprocal. Lyricist Nick Ashford, as sung by Marvin Gaye to Tammi Terrell: "Like an eagle protects his nest, / for you I'll do my best, / Stand by you like a tree, / And dare anybody to try and move me."

The best of Motown navigates the narrow passage between sophisticated linguistic expression and popular tastes, one obscure metaphor too many, and the audience vanishes. Popular music, by definition, speaks the common tongue. But an overdose of cliché guarantees a song will not survive beyond the moment. Like Billy Strayhorn and Lorenz Hart, the writers of Motown knew that a well-timed intelligent phrase was the soul of cool. It was sexy as hell. It played both in the housing projects and in Peoria: "I did you wrong. / My heart went out to play. / But in the game I lost you. / What a price to pay."

This was soul music, sensual and sweet and unafraid to display its affection publicly. Much of it may have been created in the midst of the bare-knuckles brawl that was, and is, urban life, but the music transcended bitterness in favor of life-affirming dignity. Barrett Strong, who cowrote, among others, "Just My Imagination" and "I Heard It Through the Grapevine," cites "real life" as his inspiration: "Most of us came from homes where there was a sense of family and optimism." There was always the whispering sage. Mama said, "You can't hurry love" and "You better shop around." The songs were girded by an African American ethic of grace in romance: Beauty's only skin deep, wait patiently for the real thing.

America was enchanted. The Supremes graced the cover of *Time* magazine. When the Motown tours went international, European teenagers, who had learned English by singing along with the records, enthusiastically delivered background vocals from the audience. Musical artists from every quarter spoke of Motown with admiration bordering on reverence. The Beatles, Laura Nyro, and James Taylor, master songwriters themselves, recorded Motown songs. Bob Dylan spoke of Smokey Robinson as "the greatest living American poet." Singer-songwriter Jackson Browne compared the songs to the era's engineering marvels produced in Detroit's auto plants. Indeed, the best Motown songs are masterpieces of design. Like Oscar Hammerstein and Cole Porter, these songwriters could tell a story in Technicolor. You were given a private tour of the "seven rooms of gloom," invited to "walk the land of broken dreams," huddle "in the shadows of love," or were shown "a green oasis where there's only sand." The songs were often Greek drama in miniature; you understood what a mess the singer was in, but you also knew he caused it. Hubris was inevitably followed by some humbling comeuppance. Men who thought they had a woman dangling on a string were beaten to the punch and dismissed. Hunters were captured by the game.

In the 1950s, three chords ruled pop music, but these writers served up a Crayola box of harmonic colors. Songs such as "For Once in My Life," "Reflections," and "You're All I Need to Get By" displayed a broad harmonic vocabulary without an air of pretension—like the guy who can walk into a barbershop, use words like *pedantic*, and still be one of the fellas. Products of the Detroit public schools' then legendary music program and neighborhood joints that still featured live jazz, the Motown songwriters knew song structure from way back. They could back cycle, dangle a plagal cadence, modulate, and flash a little chromaticism without breaking a sweat. When only two chords were needed to get the job done, they could weld C-sharp and F-sharp together so tightly they flowed with the inevitability of night into day. It sounded as if they were the first to discover a simple triad. The Motown songwriters instinctively understood the irreducible principle of writing anything: have something to say, say it, and stop. These writers delivered concise points of view, equal parts declarative and metaphorical: The average length of a Motown hit song between 1963 and 1968 is less than three minutes. The ghetto Zen masters set out the rules of love from the practical to the ethereal as if under the watchful eye of the haiku police. You were advised to ignore friends' advice if love hung in the balance, reassured that pretty girls were a dime a dozen, and emboldened that with a true heart you could still win the girl even if you didn't have a dime.

The musicians, not technically composers, contributed themes that became inseparable from the songs themselves. They echoed the lyrics with uncanny wordless precision. James Jamerson strung together bass lines of Morse code; you could hear Mama's relentless "Love don't come easy, / it's a game of give and take." William "Benny" Benjamin introduced tunes with signature drum lines you couldn't imagine the song without. Even the baritone saxophone, a Snuffleupagus of an instrument, sounded hip. These musicians could have gotten people up on the dance floor with a chorus of tubas.

Through the funk, innocence percolated to the surface with birdlike girl singers and the nimble percussion of pizzicato. There were finger snaps against a backdrop of symphony strings. This was music full with anticipation. The days had faded when bluesmen painted the Delta with hard times and hellhounds. These were the '60s. There was talk of living where you wanted, getting jobs because you were qualified, and looking a white man in the eye without risking your life. Mr. Gordy *owned* the record company. Integration was one thing, freedom was another. When in 1964, Sam Cooke sang "Change Is Gonna Come" on the *Tonight Show*, it sounded like the words of a prophet.

As early as the mid 1950s, the nation's vast educational resources had begun to trickle into previously neglected neighborhoods. Smokey Robinson traces his interest in language and composition to the Young Writers' Club, an after-school workshop convened by Ms. Harris, a visionary elementary school teacher. By the 1960s, a belief and investment in the untapped resources of marginalized Americans was becoming an article of faith. Programs from Leonard Bernstein's Young Peoples' Concerts to Head Start recognized that by denying opportunity to these communities the nation had robbed itself of untold contributions in science, art, and culture. The concept of a Great Society gained currency. On the neighborhood level, the Detroit public schools taught music theory, composition, and performance as if they mattered. The pace of social change was accelerated in the 1960s. What had been incremental and generational now arrived in clusters. In January of 1963, as Motown began to dominate the pop charts, a sixteen-year-old André Watts, substituting for an ailing Glenn Gould, walked onto the stage at Lincoln Center and delivered, note perfect, Liszt's E-flat Concerto. In 1964, as Motown's grip on the charts tightened, a fresh-faced Cassius Clay thanked America to refer to him henceforth as Muhammad Ali. Berry Gordy brought composers, lyricists, singers, and musicians together with his own defiant gospel of optimism and a belief that with opportunity and a forum for expression there were no limits to what could be accomplished. Their music was part flower-pushing-through-cracks in the concrete and part root shattering it.

The fleeting age of innocence and hope gave way to summers of discontent, and in an act of collective self-immolation black neighborhoods from Watts to Detroit were consumed in flame. A series of events conspired to dismantle the delicate, cautiously entertained aspirations. The descent was punctuated by the assassination of the messengers of change: Malcolm X, John and Robert Kennedy, and Medgar Evers. With the election of Richard Nixon by a silent majority that dismissed social programs as the product of a bleeding heart, reality fell far short of the vision. Hope withered. But for a time the sense of optimism in music held fast. Then, on a spring morning in 1968, word came from Memphis that Martin Luther King Jr. had been shot. The blues were back. As in the old Ellington hook, black America struggled to keep the song from going out of its heart. Within black songwriting the battle had begun between romance and rump shaking. Defeatism is anathema to art. After what happened to Martin, it seemed that only a fool could believe.

Within months of the King assassination, the Temptations' "Cloud Nine" stripped the veneer of hope and exposed a reality that could be tolerated only through a cloud of marijuana smoke. This moment was more about raw reality than idealized love. From "Ball of Confusion" to "Papa Was a Rollin' Stone" and "Run Away Child (Running Wild)," the promise of a black Camelot settled into sullen defiance. When it came to love, male vulnerability was no longer an option. In "Uptight (Everything's Alright)," Stevie Wonder once bragged that he was the apple of his girl's eye, even though the only shirt he owned was hangin' on his back. Soon a caricature of masculinity would dominate black music. Why contemplate the way to a woman's heart when you could dazzle her with *your* jewelry, a block-long car, and a wad of cash? In the coming decades, music education was phased out of many of the public schools. Those with talent learned to use turntables to scratch out a new beat. Seduced by the illusion of props, a new generation of writers confused bluster with strength and manhood with an impenetrable heart. Smokey Robinson wrote of love for a woman as "a rosebud blooming in the warmth of the summer sun." But as the African American tradition of romance faded from the music, a woman was more likely to be reduced to her anatomical components.

Still, the legacy of discipline and creative inspiration that defined the early days of Motown is manifest on Marvin Gaye's *What's Going On* and in a series of albums by Stevie Wonder culminating in *Songs in the Key of Life*. The teenage apostles of boy-girl love became standard-bearers of a spiritual, universal love. For them, soul music had evolved into music of the soul. Their lyrics have become sacred text: "War is not the answer, for only love can conquer hate," "Love's in need of love today." As did John Lennon with "Imagine" and John Coltrane with *A Love Supreme*, they looked beyond the personal and dreamed.

A Stevie Wonder lyric lamented that love had taken flight "and then a half a mile from heaven" dropped him back to this cold world. Motown's songs of romance ascended with the promise of change and faded with the onset of cynicism. In the process, the music was itself transformative, inspiring a community defined not by geography, class, or race but by a sense of common experience. The gospel of change that ignited the love affair in black music may have diminished, but for an incandescent moment, Motown celebrated life and love. No one who hears it will ever forget.

lessons of love

all in love is fair (Stevie Wonder)

Stevie Wonder

All is fair in love,
Love's a crazy game.
Two people vow to stay
In love as one, they say.
But all is changed with time,
The future none can see.
The road you leave behind,
Ahead lies mystery.
But all is fair in love,
I had to go away.
A writer takes his pen
To write the words again,
That all in love is fair.

All of fate's a chance,
It's either good or bad.
I tossed my coin to say
In love with me you'd stay.
But all in war is so cold,
You either win or lose.
When all is put away,
The losing side I'll play.
But all is fair in love,
I should have never left your side.
A writer takes his pen
To write the words again,
That all in love is fair.

A writer takes his pen
To write the words again,
That all in love is fair.

ask the lonely (Ivy Jo Hunter, William "Mickey" Stevenson)

The Four Tops

Just ask the lonely.

When you feel that you
Can make it all alone,
Remember no one is big enough to
Go it alone.

Just ask the lonely,
They know the hurt and pain
Of losing a love you can never regain.

Just ask the lonely,
Just ask the lonely.

The young and foolish laugh at love,
And so they run away,
Confident and sure that fate
Will bring another love their way.

But ask the lonely,
How vainly a heart can yearn
For losing a love that will never return.

Just ask the lonely,
Just ask the lonely.

They'll tell you,
They'll tell you a story of sadness,
A story too hard to believe . . .
They'll tell you the loneliest one is me,
Just ask the lonely,
Just ask the lonely.

Ask me,
I'm the loneliest one you'll see.
Just ask.
I'm the loneliest one you will see.

back in my arms again (Edward Holland Jr., Lamont Dozier, Brian Holland)

The Supremes

All day long I hear my telephone ring,
Friends calling, giving their advice.
From the boy I love, I should break away,
'Cause heartaches he'll bring one day.

I lost him once through friends' advice,
But it's not gonna happen twice.
'Cause all advice's ever gotten me
Was many long and sleepless nights.

But now he's back in my arms again,
Right by my side.
I got him back in my arms again,
So satisfied.

It's easy for friends to say let him go,
But I'm the one who needs him so.
It's his love that makes me strong,
Without him I can't go on.
This time I'll live my life at ease,
Being happy, lovin' whom I please.
And each time we make romance,
I'll be thankful for a second chance.

'Cause he's back in my arms again,
Right by my side.
I got him back in my arms again,
So satisfied.

How can Mary tell me what to do
When she lost her love so true?
And Flo, she don't know,
'Cause the boy she loves is a Romeo.
I listened once to my friends' advice,
But it's not gonna happen twice.
'Cause all advice ever got me
Was many long and sleepless nights.

Ooh! I got him back in my arms again,
Right by my side.
I got him back in my arms again,
So satisfied.
I'm satisfied,
So satisfied.
I'm satisfied,
I'm satisfied.

beauty is only skin deep (Edward Holland Jr., Norman Whitfield)

The Temptations

So in love, sad as can be,
'Cause her pretty face got the best of me.
Suddenly you came into my life,
And gave it meaning and pure delight.
Now good looks I've learned to do without,
'Cause now I know it's love that really counts.

'Cause I know that
Beauty's only skin deep, yeah, yeah, yeah,
Beauty's only skin deep, oh yeah.

Now you speak your words warm and sincere,
And lets me know your love is dear.
A pretty face you may not possess,
But what I like about you is your tenderness.
A pretty face may be some guys' taste,
But I'll take lovin' in its place.

'Cause I know that
Beauty's only skin deep, yeah, yeah, yeah,
And you know that
Beauty's only skin deep, oh yeah.

My friends ask what do I see in you,
But it goes deeper than the eye can view.
You have a pleasing personality,
And that's an ever-lovin' rare quality.
Now show me a girl, a girl that's fine,
And I'll choose the one with true lovin' every time.

'Cause I know that
Beauty's only skin deep, yeah, yeah, yeah,
And I believe that
Beauty's only skin deep, oh yeah.

So if you're looking for a lover
Oh yeah
Don't judge book by its cover
Oh yeah

She may be fine on the outside
Oh yeah
But so untrue on the inside.

does your mama know about me? (Tom Baird, Tommy Chong)

Bobby Taylor and The Vancouvers

Does your mama know about me?
Does she know just what I am?
Will she turn her back on me,
Or accept me as a man?

And what about your dad?
Did you think of what he'll say?
Will he be understanding,
Or does he think the usual way?

Maybe I shouldn't worry,
But I've been through this before.
And I'd like to get things straight
Before I'm knocking on your door.

Does your mama know about me?
Does she know just what I am?
If she says forget about me,
Do you think you'll understand?

And what about your friends?
Do you care what people say?
Will you accept the burdens
I know will surely come your way?

Maybe I shouldn't worry,
But I've been through this before.
And I'd like to get things straight
Before I'm knocking on your door.

Does your mama know about me?
Does she know just what I am?
Will she turn her back on me,
Or accept me as a man?

We've got to stand tall,
Not tumble or fall.
We've got to be strong
For a love that's so right,
Can't be wrong.

And every day I see it grow,
And I don't want to let it go.
I guess that's why I've got to know,
Does your mama know about me?
Does your mama know about me?

don't look back (William "Smokey" Robinson, Ronald White)

The Temptations

If it's love that you're running from, there's no hiding place.
Love has problems, I know, but they're problems
    we'll just have to face.

If you just put your hand in mine,
We're gonna leave all our troubles behind.
We're gonna walk and don't look back, don't look back,
And don't look back,
And don't look back, baby, don't look back.
The past is behind you, let nothing remind you.

If your first lover broke your heart,
There's something that can be done.
Don't end your faith in love because of what he's done.

So if you just put your hand in mine,
We're gonna leave all our troubles behind.
Keep on walking, don't look back, don't look back.
Forget about the past now,
Don't look back, baby.
Keep on walking, and don't look back, hmm.
The past is behind you, let nothing remind you.

Love can be a beautiful thing,
Though your first love let you down.
'Cause I know we can make love bloom, baby,
The second time around.

So if you just put your hand in mine,
We're gonna leave all our troubles behind.
Keep on pushing and don't look back.
Now, 'til I say, we won't look back, girl.
Keep on walking and won't look back.
Forget about the past now, baby,
And don't look back.

the hunter gets captured by the game (William "Smokey" Robinson)

The Marvelettes

Every day things change
And the world puts on a new face.
Certain things rearrange
And this old world seems like a new place.

Oh yeah, secretly I've been trailing you
Like a fox that preys on the rabbit.
I had to get you, and so I knew
I had to learn your ways and habits.

Ooo, you were the catch that I was after,
But I looked up and I was in your arms,
And I knew I had been captured.

What's this old world coming to?
Things just ain't the same
Any time the hunter gets captured by the game, oh yeah.

Oh yeah, I had laid such a tender trap,
Hopin' you might fall into it.
But love hit me like a sudden slap,
One kiss, then I knew it.

Ooo, my plan didn't work out like I thought,
'Cause I had laid my trap for you,
But it seems like I got caught.

What's this old world coming to?
Things just ain't the same
Any time the hunter gets captured by the game, oh yeah, oh yeah.

if it's magic (Stevie Wonder)

Stevie Wonder

If it's magic . . .
Then why can't it be everlasting,
Like the sun that always shines,
Like the poet's endless rhyme,
Like the galaxies in time?

If it's pleasing . . .
Then why can't it be never leaving,
Like the day that never fails,
Like on seashores there are shells,
Like the time that always tells?

It holds the key to every heart
Throughout the universe.
It fills you up without a bite,
And quenches every thirst.

So . . .
If it's special,
Then with it why aren't we as careful
As making sure we dress in style,
Posing pictures with a smile,
Keeping danger from a child?

It holds the key to every heart
Throughout the universe.
It fills you up without a bite,
And quenches every thirst.

So . . .
If it's magic . . .
Why can't we make it everlasting,
Like the lifetime of the sun?
It will leave no heart undone,
For there's enough for everyone.

i'll be doggone (Warren "Pete" Moore, William "Smokey" Robinson, Marvin Tarplin)

Marvin Gaye

Well, I'd be doggone if I wouldn't work all day,
And I'd be doggone if I wouldn't bring you my pay.
But if I ever caught you running around,
Blowing my money all over this town,

Then I wouldn't be doggone,
Hey, hey, I'd be long gone.
Then I wouldn't be doggone,
I'd be long gone.

I'll be doggone if you ain't a pretty thing,
And I'll be doggone if you ain't warm as a breath of spring.
And if we live to be a hundred years old,
If you ever let that spring turn cold,

Then I wouldn't be doggone,
Hey, hey, hey, I'll be long gone.
Oh, I wouldn't be doggone, baby,
I'd be long gone.

Now did you hear me?
Well now, what I say,
Oh, believe me.

Well, every woman should try
To be whatever her man wants her to be.
And I don't want much,
All I want from you is for you to be true to me.

I'll be doggone if love ain't a man's best friend, oh baby,
And I'll be doggone if you ain't the loving end.
Though I know you make me feel like nobody could
If I ever found out that you're no good,

Then I wouldn't be doggone,
I'd be long gone.
Well, I wouldn't be doggone, baby,
I'd be long gone.

it takes two (Sylvia Moy, William "Mickey" Stevenson)

Marvin Gaye and Kim Weston

Kim: One can have a dream, baby,
Marvin: Two can make that dream so real.
Kim: One can talk about being in love,
Marvin: Two can say how it really feels.
Kim: One can wish upon a star,
Marvin: Two can make that wish come true, yeah.
Kim: One can stand alone in the dark,
Marvin: Two can make the light shine through.

Both: It takes two, baby, It takes two, baby,
Me and you, just takes two.
It takes two, baby, It takes two, baby,
To make a dream come true, it just takes two.

Kim: One can have a broken heart, livin' in misery,
Marvin: Two can really ease the pain like a perfect remedy.
Kim: One can be alone in a crowd, like an island he's all alone,
Marvin: Two can make just anyplace seem just like being at home.

Both: It takes two, baby, It takes two, baby,
Me and you, just takes two.
It takes two, baby, It takes two, baby,
To make a dream come true, it just takes two.

Kim: One can go out to a movie, lookin' for a special treat,
Marvin: Two can make that single movie
somethin' really kinda sweet.
Kim: One can take a walk in the moonlight,
thinkin' that it's really nice,
Marvin: But two walkin' hand in hand
is like addin' just a pinch of spice.

Both: It takes two, baby, It takes two, baby,
Me and you, it just takes two.
It takes two, baby, It takes two, baby,
To make a dream come true, it just takes two.

the love i saw in you was just a mirage (William "Smokey" Robinson, Marvin Tarplin)

Smokey Robinson and the Miracles

There you were, beautiful,
The promise of love was written on your face.
You led me on with untrue kisses,
Oh, you held me captive in your false embrace.
Quicker than I could bat an eye,
Seems you were telling me goodbye.

Just a minute ago your love was here,
All of a sudden it seemed to disappear.
Sweetness was only heartache's camouflage,
The love I saw in you was just a mirage.

We used to meet in romantic places,
Oh, you gave the illusion that your love was real.
Now all that's left are lipstick traces
From the kisses you only pretended to feel.
And now our meetings you avoid,
And so my world you have destroyed.

Just a minute ago your love was here,
All of a sudden it seemed to disappear, yeah.
The way you wrecked my life was like sabotage,
The love I saw in you was just a mirage.

You only filled me with despair
By showin' love that wasn't there.

Just like the desert shows a thirsty man
A green oasis where there's only sand,
You lured me into something I should have dodged,
The love I saw in you was just a mirage.

the love you save (The Corporation: Berry Gordy Jr., Alphonso Mizell, Freddie Perren, Deke Richards)

The Jackson 5

Stop, stop, stop, you'd better save it.
Stop, stop, stop, you'd better save it.

When we played tag in grade school,
You wanted to be It.
But chasing boys was just a fad,
You crossed your heart, you'd quit.

When we grew up, you traded
Your promise for my ring.
Now just like back to grade school,
You're doing the same old thing.

Stop! The love you save may be your own.
Darling, take it slow,
Or someday you'll be all alone.
You'd better stop, the love you save may be your own.
Darling, look both ways before you cross me,
You're headed for the danger zone.

I'm the one who loves you,
I'm the one you need.
Those other guys will put you down
As soon as they succeed.

They'll ruin your reputation,
They'll label you a flirt.
The way they talk about you,
They'll turn your name to dirt, oh.

Isaac said he kissed you
Beneath the apple tree.
When Benjie held your hand, he felt
Electricity.
When Alexander called you,
He said he rang your chimes.
Christopher discovered
You're way ahead of your time.

Stop! The love you save may be your own.
Darling, take it slow,
Or someday you'll be all alone.
You'd better stop! The love you save may be your own.
Darling, look both ways before you cross me,
You're headed for a danger zone.

Slow down,
Slow down,
Slow down,
Slow down.

S is for "Save it,"
T is for "Take it slow,"
O is for "Oh, no,"
P is for "Please, please don't go!"

The love you save may be your own . . .
Someday you may be all alone . . .

Stop it, save it, girl,
Baby, ooo.
You better stop—the love you save may be your own,
Please, please,
Or someday, someday, baby,
You'll be all alone.

I'm the one who loves you,
I'm the one you need.
Those other guys will put you down as soon as they succeed.

Stop! The love you save may be your own, baby,
You'd better stop it, stop it, stop it, girl,
Or someday you'll be all alone.
The way they talk about you,
They'll turn your name to dirt.

Stop! The love you save may be your own.
Don'tcha know, don'tcha know,
Someday, baby, you'll be all alone.
Those other guys will put you down as soon as they succeed.

shop around (Berry Gordy Jr., William "Smokey" Robinson)

Smokey Robinson and The Miracles

When I became of age, my mother called me to her side.
She said, Son, you're growing up now. Pretty soon you'll take a bride.
And then she said,
Just because you've become a young man now,
There's still some things that you don't understand now.
Before you ask some girl for her hand now,
Keep your freedom for as long as you can now.

My mama told me, You better shop around,
You better shop around.

There's some things that I want you to know now,
Just as sure as the wind's gonna blow now,
The women come and the women gonna go now,
Before you tell 'em that you love 'em so now.

My mama told me, You better shop around,
You better shop around.

Try to get yourself a bargain, son,
Don't be sold on the very first one.
Pretty girls come a dime a dozen,
Try to find one who's gonna give ya true lovin'.
Before you take a girl and say I do, now,
Make sure she's in love a-with you now.
My mama told me, You better shop around.

Try to get yourself a bargain, son,
Don't be sold on the very first one.
Pretty girls come a dime a dozen,
Try to find one who's gonna give ya true lovin'.
Before you take a girl and say, I do, now,
Make sure she's in love with you now,
Make sure that her love is true now,
I'd hate to see you feelin' sad and blue now.
My mama told me, You better shop around.

Don't let the first one get you.
Oh no, 'cause I don't wanna see her with you,

Before you let 'em hold you tight
Yeah, yeah make sure she's all right.
Uh-huh, before you let her take your hand, my son,
Understand, my son,
Be a man, my son,
I know you can, my son,
I love it . . . a-shop around.

uptight (everything's all right) (Henry Cosby, Sylvia Moy, Stevie Wonder)

Stevie Wonder

Baby, everything is all right, uptight, out of sight.
Baby, everything is all right, uptight, out of sight.

I'm a poor man's son, from across the railroad tracks,
The only shirt I own is hangin' on my back.
But I'm the envy of every single guy
Since I'm the apple of my girl's eye.
When we go out stepping on the town for awhile,
My money's low and my suits are out of style.

But it's all right if my clothes aren't new,
Out of sight, because my heart is true.
She says, baby, everything is all right, uptight, out of sight,
Baby, everything is all right, uptight, clean out of sight.

She's a pearl of a girl, I guess that's what you might say,
I guess her folks brought her up that way.
The right side of the tracks, she was born and raised
In a great big old house, full of butlers and maids.
She said, no one is better than I,
I know I'm just an average guy.

No football hero or smooth Don Juan,
Got empty pockets, you see, I'm a poor man's son.
Can't give her the things that money can buy,
But I'll never, never, never make my baby cry.

And it's all right, what I can't do,
Out of sight, because my heart is true.
She says, baby, everything is all right, uptight, clean out of sight,
Baby, everything is all right, uptight, clean out of sight,
Baby, everything is all right, uptight,
Baby, everything is all right, uptight, way out of sight,
Baby, everything is all right, uptight, clean out of sight.

you beat me to the punch (William "Smokey" Robinson, Ronald White)

Mary Wells

That day I first saw you, passing by,
I wanted to know your name, but I was much too shy.
But I was looking at you so hard
That you must have had a hunch.
So you came up to me and asked me my name.

You beat me to the punch
That time,
You beat me to the punch,
You beat me to the punch.

After I hadn't known you for what seems like a long, long time,
I wanted, wanted to ask you, would you please, please be mine?
Whenever you came around, my heart would pound,
So you must have had a hunch.
So you came up to me, you asked me to be yours.

You beat me to the punch
One more time,
You beat me to the punch,
You beat me to the punch.

Since I loved you,
I thought you would be true
And love me tender.
So I let my heart surrender
To you, yes, I did.
But I found out
Beyond a doubt
One day, boy,
You were a playboy
Who would go away and leave me
Blue.

So I ain't gonna wait around for you to put me down.
This time I'm gonna play my hunch
And walk away this very day,
And beat you to the punch.

This time
I'll beat you to the punch, yes I will.
Let you know, know how it feels.

you can't hurry love (Edward Holland Jr., Lamont Dozier, Brian Holland)

The Supremes

I need love, love
To ease my mind.
I need to find, find
Someone to call mine.

But Mama said,
You can't hurry love,
No, you just have to wait.
She said love don't come easy,
It's a game of give and take.

You can't hurry love,
No, you just have to wait.
You got to trust, give it time,
No matter how long it takes.

But how many heartaches
Must I stand before I find a love
To let me live again.
Right now the only thing
That keeps me hangin' on
When I feel my strength, yeah,
It's almost gone.

I remember, Mama said,
You can't hurry love,
No, you just have to wait.
She said love don't come easy,
It's a game of give and take.

How long must I wait,
How much more can I take,
Before loneliness will cause my heart, heart to break.

No, I can't bear to live my life alone,
I grow impatient for a love to call my own.
But when I feel that I, I can't go on,
These precious words keeps me hangin' on.

I remember, Mama said,
You can't hurry love,
No, you just have to wait.
She said love don't come easy,
It's a game of give and take.

You can't hurry love,
No, you just have to wait.
She said trust, give it time,
No matter how long it takes.

No, love, love, don't come easy,
But I keep on waiting,
Anticipating,
For that soft voice
To talk to me at night,
For some tender arms
To hold me tight.
I keep waiting,
I keep on waiting,
But it ain't easy,
It ain't easy.

But Mama said,
You can't hurry love,
No, you just have to wait.
She said trust, give it time,
No matter how long it takes.

You can't hurry love,
No, you just have to wait.
She said love don't come easy,
It's a game of give and take.

when i'm gone (William "Smokey" Robinson)

Mary Wells

What are you gonna do when I'm gone?
Whose shoulder are you gonna cry on?
What are you gonna do on the day
When I turn my head and just walk away, now?
What are you gonna say to your friends
When the talk around town begins?
Will you tell them how you treated me bad?
Will you tell them how you made me so sad?

You make some people think that you love me a lot,
They just don't know you,
What they see isn't what we've got.

We're happy in the public eye,
They think you're such a wonderful guy.
But they don't know how much you've lied,
And they don't know how much I've cried.
You're a real Dr. Jekyll/Mr. Hyde.

You make a pass at
Every girl that you see.
Then when they hurt you,
You come right back crying to me.
I comfort you whenever you're low,
And you don't have a place to go.
You put your head on my shoulder and cry,
And then you turn around and tell me a lie.

And I just can't take it,
I've gotta make it.

What are you gonna do when I'm gone?
What are you gonna do when I'm gone?

the path to your heart

do you love me (Berry Gordy Jr.)

The Contours

Spoken: You broke my heart,
'Cause I couldn't dance.
You didn't even want me around.
And now I'm back to let you know
I can really shake 'em down.

Sung: Do you love me? I can really move.
Do you love me? I'm in the groove.
Ah, do you love? Do you love me?
Now that I can dance, dance, dance.

Watch me now, hey — work, work.
Ah, work it out, baby — work, work.
Well you're driving me crazy — work, work.
With just a little bit of soul now — work.

I can mash-potato,
   I can mash-potato,
And do the twist,
   I can do the twist.
Now tell me, baby,
   Tell me, baby,
Do you like it like this?
   Do you like it like this?
Tell me, tell me, tell me.

Do you love me?
   Do you love me?
Now, do you love me?
   Do you love me?
Now, do you love me?
   Do you love me?
Now that I can dance, dance, dance.

Watch me now, hey — work, work.
Oh shake it up, shake it — work, work
Ah, shake it, shake 'em down — work, work.
Ah, a little bit of soul, now — work.
Ah, getting it, baby.

Ah, you're right with it, baby—work, work
Ah, don't get lazy—work.

I can mash-potato,
   I can mash-potato,
And do the twist,
   I can do the twist.
Now tell me, baby,
   Tell me, baby,
Do you like it like this?
   Do you like it like this?
Tell me, tell me, tell me.

Do you love me?
   Do you love me?
Now, do you love me?
   Do you love me?
Now, do you love me?
   Do you love me?
Now that I can dance?

get ready (William "Smokey" Robinson)

The Temptations

I never met a girl who makes me feel the way that you do—
    you're all right.
Whenever I'm asked who makes my dreams real, I say that you do—
    you're outta sight.

So, fee-fi-fo-fum,
Look out, baby, 'cause here I come.

And I'm bringing you a love that's true,
So get ready, so get ready.
I'm gonna try to make you love me too,
So get ready, so get ready, 'cause here I come.

Get ready, 'cause here I come,
I'm on my way,
Get ready, 'cause here I come.

If you wanna play hide and seek with love, let me remind you—
    it's all right.
But the lovin' you're gonna miss in the time it takes to find you—
    it's outta sight.

So, fiddley-dee, fiddley-dum,
Look out, baby, 'cause here I come.

And I'm bringing you a love that's true,
So get ready, so get ready.
I'm gonna try to make you love me too,
So get ready, so get ready, 'cause here I come.

Get ready, 'cause here I come,
I'm on my way,
Get ready, 'cause here I come,
Get ready.

If all my friends should want you too, I'll understand it—
    be all right.
I hope I get to you before they do, the way I planned it—
    be outta sight.

So twiddley-dee, twiddley-dum,
Look out, baby, 'cause here I come.

And I'm bringing you a love that's true,
So get ready, so get ready.
I'm gonna try to make you love me too,
So get ready, so get ready, 'cause here I come.

Get ready, 'cause here I come,
I'm on my way,
Get ready, 'cause here I come.

he was really sayin' somthin' (Edward Holland Jr., Norman Whitfield, William "Mickey" Stevenson)

The Velvelettes

I was walking down the street
When this boy started following me.
Though I ignored all the things he said,
He moved me in every way.

With his collar unbuttoned,
By my side he was struttin'.
Girls, he was really sayin' somthin'.

Girls, he flirted every step of the way,
I could feel every word he'd say.
My resistance was getting low,
And my feelings were starting to show.
My heart started thumpin',
Blood pressure jumpin'.

Girls, he was really sayin' somthin',
Really sayin' somthin'.

As he walked me to my door,
I agreed to see him once more.
Ladylike, it may not be, no,
But he moved me tremendously.

Though he was bold, my heart he stole.
Girls, he was really sayin' somthin',
Really sayin' somthin'.

hitch hike (Marvin Gaye, Clarence Paul, William "Mickey" Stevenson)

Marvin Gaye

I'm goin' to Chicago, that's the last place my baby strayed.
Hitch hike, hitch hike, baby.
I'm packin' up my bags; gonna leave this old town right away.
Hitch hike, hitch hike, baby.
I've got to find that girl, if I have to hitch hike 'round the world.
Hitch hike, hitch hike.

Chicago City Limits, that's what the sign on the highway read.
Hitch hike, hitch hike, baby.
I'm gonna keep movin' 'til I get to that street corner, Sixth and Third.
Hitch hike, hitch hike, yeah.
I've got to find that girl, if I have to hitch hike 'round the world.
Hitch hike, hitch hike, baby.

Hitch hike, now hitch-a hike,
Hitch a ride, hitch hike, children.
Hitch hike, hitch hike,
Yeah, hitch hike, hitch hike, children.

Hitch hike, baby, hitch hike, children
Hitch hike, baby, hitch hike, children
Hitch hike, baby, hitch hike, baby.

I'm goin' to St. Louis, but my next stop just might be L.A.
Now what'd I say?
Got no money in my pocket, so I'm gonna have to
    hitch hike all the way.
Yeah.
I've got to find that girl, if I have to hitch hike 'round the world.
Now what'd I say?

Come on, hitch hike,
Come hitch hike, children . . .

i'll try something new (William "Smokey" Robinson)

Smokey Robinson and the Miracles

I will build you a castle with a tower so high
It reaches the moon.
I'll gather melodies from birdies that fly,
And compose you a tune.
Give you lovin' warm as Mama's oven and
If that don't do, then I'll try something new.

I will take you away with me as far as I can,
To Venus or Mars.
There we will love with your hand in my hand,
You'll be queen of the stars.
And every day we can play on the Milky Way and
If that don't do, then I'll try something new.

I will bring you a flower from the floor of the sea,
To wear in your hair.
I'll do anything and everything to keep you happy,
Girl, to show you that I care.
I'll pretend I'm jealous of all the fellas and
If that don't do, then I'll try something new.

I'd take the stars and count them
And move a mountain
And if that don't do,
I'll try something new,

On the moon above
I'll write it's you I love.
And baby, if it don't do
I'm gonna try something new.

If at first I don't succeed
Try again is what I'll do.
Always tryin' something else,
Always trying something that's new.

i'm gonna make you love me (Kenneth Gamble, Jerry Ross, Leon Huff)

The Supremes and The Temptations

I'm gonna do all the things for you
A girl wants a man to do.
Oh, baby.
I'll sacrifice for you,
I'll even do wrong for you.
Oh, baby.

Every minute, every hour,
I'm gonna shower you
With love and affection.
Look out, it's comin' in your direction.

And I'm gonna make you love me,
Oh, yes, I will,
Yes, I will.
I'm gonna make you love me,
Oh, yes, I will,
Yes, I will.

Look here,
My love is strong, you see.
I know you'll never get tired of me.
Oh, baby.

And I'm gonna use every trick in the book,
I'll try my best to get you hooked.
Hey, baby.

And every night, every day,
I'm gonna say,
I'm gonna get you, I'm gonna get you,
Look out, boy, 'cause I'm gonna get you.

I'm gonna make you love me,
Ooo, yes, I will,
Yes, I will.
And I'm gonna make you love me,
Ooo, yes, I will,
You know I will.

Every breath I take,
And each and every step I make,
Brings me closer, baby,
Closer to you.

And with each beat of my heart,
For every day we're apart,
I'll hunger for every wasted hour.

And every night,
And every day,
I'm gonna get you, I'm gonna get you,
Look out, 'cause I'm gonna get you.

I'm gonna make you love me,
Oh, yes, I will,
Yes, I will.
I'm gonna make you love me,
Oh, yes, I will,
Yes, I will.

I'm gonna make you love me,
Oh, yes, I will,
Yes, I will.
I'm gonna make you love me,
Oh, yes, I will,
Yes, I will.

it's growing (Warren "Pete" Moore, William "Smokey" Robinson)

The Temptations

Like a snowball rolling down the side of a snow-covered hill,
It's growing.
Like the size of the fish that the man claims broke his reel,
It's growing.
Like the rosebud blooming in the warmth of the summer sun,
It's growing,
Like the tale by the time it's been told by more than one,
It's growing.

Every day it grows a little more than it was the day before.
My love for you just grows and grows,
Oh, how it grows and grows,
And where it's going to stop,
I'm sure, nobody knows.
How it grows and it grows and it grows.
Oh, yeah, yeah, yeah, yeah.
Ooo.

Like the need in a guy to see his girl when she's gone away,
It's growing.
Like the sadness in his little heart when he knows
    that she's gone to stay,
It's growing.

Every day it grows a little more than it was the day before.
My love for you just grows and grows,
Oh, how it grows and grows,
And where it's going to stop, I'm sure, nobody knows.
It gets a little wider,
It gets a little stronger,
The feeling from each kiss, baby,
It lasts a little longer.
Ooo, so much, Ooo, so much.
Can't you see it's growing, baby?
It grows and it grows and it grows.

stubborn kind of fellow (Marvin Gaye, George Gordy, William "Mickey" Stevenson)

Marvin Gaye

Say yeah yeah yeah, say yeah yeah yeah.
One more time now, baby,
Say yeah yeah yeah, say yeah yeah yeah.

I try to put my arms around you,
All because I wanna
Hold you tight.
But every time I reach for you, baby,
Try to kiss you,
You just jump clean out of sight.

Whoa, I got news for you,
Baby, now I've made plans for two.
I guess I'm just a stubborn kind of fella,
Got my mind made up to love you.

Say yeah yeah yeah, say yeah yeah yeah.

I'm gonna love you,
In every way.
I'm gonna love you,
In every way, yeah.

With other girls I've wanted,
I dated just a moment.
With you I shall remain.
Now I know you've heard about me,
Bad things about me.
Baby, please let me explain.
Oh, I have kissed a few, tell you, a few have kissed me too.

I guess I'm just a stubborn kind of fella,
Got my mind made up to love you.

Whoa, everybody sing yeah yeah yeah, yeah yeah yeah,
Whoa, everybody sing yeah yeah yeah, yeah yeah yeah,
Uh-huh-huh, sing now, everybody, yeah yeah yeah, yeah yeah yeah,
    whoa.

when the lovelight starts shining through his eyes

(Edward Holland Jr./Lamont Dozier/Brian Holland)

The Supremes

He gave me the eye
But I just passed him by.
I treated him unkind
But he didn't seem to mind.

I told him be on his way
But not a word did he say,
He just stood there kind of bold
While I acted cold.

But when the lovelight starts
Shining through his eyes
Made me realize
I should apologize.
And when he placed a kiss
Upon my face,
Then I knew, oh then I knew,
That he won my heart

So I quickly apologized
Hoping he hadn't changed his mind,
But not a word did he say
So I turned to walk away.

But when the lovelight starts
Shining through his eyes
Made me realize
How he felt inside.
And when he placed a kiss
Upon my face,
Then I knew, oh then I knew,
That he won my heart.

When he asked could he walk my way
I hoped sweet things he'd say,
Instead he smiled kinda nice
As he held my hand kinda tight.

But when the love light starts

Shining through his eyes
Made me realize
How he felt inside.
And when he placed a kiss
Upon my face . . .
Ooo Ooo.

the promise

baby i'm for real (Marvin Gaye, Anna Gaye)

The Originals

Baby, baby, you don't understand
How much I love you, baby,
How much I want to be
Your only man, oh, baby.

Baby, baby, baby, you don't have to go.
Stay a little while longer, baby.
I want to talk to you
Just a little more.

I see the little tears in your eyes about to fall.
You are wondering if I'm for real,
But if you cry, I wonder why you cry.
I tell you no lie, this is how I feel,
Baby, I'm for real.

But if you want to know the truth about it,
Girl, I just couldn't live without you.
And that's why I'm confessing my love to you,
So then I can live my whole life with you.
Darling,
Never, never, never, never going to leave you, baby.

if this world were mine (Marvin Gaye)

Marvin Gaye and Tammi Terrell

Marvin: If this world were mine,
I would place at your feet
All that I own.
You've been so good to me.
If this world were mine,
I'd give you the flowers, the birds, and the bees,
With your love beside me, that would be all I'd need.
If this world were mine,
I'd give you anything.

Tammi: If this world were mine,
I'd make you a king,
With wealth untold.
You could have anything.
If this world were mine,
I'd give you each day, so sunny and blue,
If you wanted the moonlight, I'd give you that, too.
If this world were mine,
I'd give you anything.

Marvin: Oh baby, you're my consolation,
    and there's no hesitation.
When you want me, honey, just call me.

Tammi: And you're my inspiration,
And I feel so much sensation when I'm in your arms,
When you squeeze me.

Marvin: Every sky would be blue
Long as you're loving me.

Tammi: If you're here in my arms,
Life is so wonderful.

Both: Give me plenty lovin', baby,
Give me plenty lovin', honey,
Keep on lovin' me.
Oh, you know I need you, baby,
Really, really need you, honey.

i'll be there (Hal Davis, Berry Gordy Jr., Willie Hutch, Bob West)

The Jackson 5

You and I must make a pact; we must bring salvation back.
Where there is love, I'll be there.

I'll reach out my hand to you,
I'll have faith in all you do.
Just call my name, and I'll be there.

I'll be there to comfort you,
Build my world of dreams around you, I'm so glad that I found you.
I'll be there with a love that's strong,
I'll be your strength, I'll keep holding on.

Let me fill your heart with joy and laughter.
Togetherness, girl, that's all I'm after.
Whenever you need me, I'll be there.
I'll be there to protect you, with an unselfish love that respects you.
Just call my name, and I'll be there.

I'll be there to comfort you,
Build my world of dreams around you, I'm so glad that I found you.
I'll be there with a love that's strong,
I'll be your strength, I'll keep holding on.

If you should ever find someone new,
I know he'd better be good to you,
'Cause if he doesn't, I'll be there.
Don't you know, baby, yeah, yeah,
I'll be there, I'll be there,
Just call my name, I'll be there.

Just look over your shoulder, honey, ooo.

I'll be there, I'll be there,
Whenever you need me, I'll be there,
Don't you know, baby, yeah, yeah.

I'll be there, I'll be there, just call my name, I'll be there.

reach out i'll be there (Edward Holland Jr., Lamont Dozier, Brian Holland)

The Four Tops

Now if you feel that you can't go on,
Because all of your hope is gone,
And your life is filled with much confusion,
Until happiness is just an illusion,
And your world around is crumblin' down,
Darling, reach out,
Come on, girl, reach out for me,
Reach out for me.

I'll be there with a love that will shelter you.
I'll be there with a love that will see you through.

When you feel lost and about to give up,
'Cause your best just ain't good enough.
And you feel the world has just grown cold,
And you're drifting out all on your own.
And you need a hand to hold,
Darlin', reach out,
Come on, girl, reach out for me,
Reach out for me.

I'll be there to love and comfort you,
I'll be there to cherish and care for you,
I'll be there to always see you through,
I'll be there to love and comfort you.

I can tell the way you hang your head,
You're without love now, now you're afraid,
And through your tears you look around,
But there's no peace of mind to be found.
I know what you're thinking,
You're alone now, no love of your own.
But darling, reach out,
Come on girl, reach out for me,
Reach out,
Just look over your shoulder.

I'll be there to give you all the love you need,
And I'll be there, you can always depend on me.
I'll be there.

you're all i need to get by (Nickolas Ashford, Valerie Simpson)

Marvin Gaye and Tammi Terrell

Marvin: Like the sweet morning dew,
I took one look at you,
And it was plain to see
You were my destiny.

Tammi: With arms open wide,
I threw away my pride.
I'll sacrifice for you,
Dedicate my life to you.
I will go where you lead,
Always there in time of need.

Marvin: There when I lose my will,
You'll be there to push me up the hill.

Both: There's no, no looking back for us,
We got love, sure 'nough, that's enough.
You're all, you're all I need to get by.

Marvin: Like an eagle protects his nest,
For you I'll do my best,
Stand by you like a tree,
And dare anybody to try and move me.

Tammi: Darling, in you I found
Strength where I was torn down.
Don't know what's in store,
But together we can open any door,
Just to do what's good for you, and inspire you a little higher.

Marvin: I know you can make a man
    out of a soul that didn't have a goal.

Both: 'Cause we, we got the right foundation and with love and
    determination
You're all, you're all I want to strive for, and do a little more.
You're all, all the joys under the sun wrapped up into one.
You're all, you're all I need,
You're all I need,
You're all I need, to get by.

the joy of love

ain't no mountain high enough (Nickolas Ashford, Valerie Simpson)

Marvin Gaye and Tammi Terrell

Marvin: Listen baby.
Ain't no mountain high,
Ain't no valley low,
Ain't no river wide enough, baby.

Tammi: If you need me, call me,
No matter where you are,
No matter how far.

Marvin: Don't worry, baby,

Tammi: Just call my name,
I'll be there in a hurry,
You don't have to worry.

Both: 'Cause, baby,
There ain't no mountain high enough,
Ain't no valley low enough,
Ain't no river wide enough,
To keep me from getting to you, babe.

Marvin: Remember the day
I set you free,
I told you could always count on me, darling.
From that day on, I made a vow,
I'll be there when you want me,
Some way, somehow.

Both: Oh, baby,
There ain't no mountain high enough,
Ain't no valley low enough,
Ain't no river wide enough,
To keep me from getting to you, babe.

Marvin: Oh no, darling.

Tammi: No wind, no rain,
Or winter's cold,
Can stop me, baby

Marvin: No, no, baby,

Tammi: 'Cause you are my goal.

Marvin: If you're ever in trouble,
I'll be there on the double,
Just send for me,

Both: Oh, baby.

Tammi: My love is alive
Way down in my heart,
Although we are miles apart.

Marvin: If you ever need a helping hand,
I'll be there on the double,
Just as fast as I can.

Both: Don't you know that
There ain't no mountain high enough,
Ain't no valley low enough,
Ain't no river wide enough,

Tammi: To keep me from getting to you, babe.

Both: Don't you know that there ain't no mountain high enough,
Ain't no valley low enough,
Ain't no river wide enough.
Ain't no mountain high enough,
Ain't no valley low enough.

ain't nothing like the real thing (Nickolas Ashford, Valerie Simpson)

Marvin Gaye and Tammi Terrell

Both: Ain't nothing like the real thing, baby,
Ain't nothing like the real thing.
Ain't nothing like the real thing, baby,
Ain't nothing like the real thing.

Tammi: I got your picture hangin' on the wall.
But it can't see or come to me when I call your name.
I realize it's just a picture in a frame.

Marvin: I read your letters when you're not near,
But they don't move me,
And they don't groove me like when I hear
Your sweet voice whispering in my ear.

Both: Ain't nothing like the real thing, baby,
Ain't nothing like the real thing.

Tammi: I play my game, a fantasy.
I pretend, but I know in reality.
I need the shelter of your arms to comfort me.

Both: No other sound is quite the same as your name,
No touch can do half as much.

Marvin: To make me feel better,

Tammi: So let's stay together.

Marvin: I got some memories to look back on,
Though they help me when you phone,
I'm well aware nothing can take the place of being there.

Both: So glad we got the real thing, baby,
So glad we got the real thing.
Ain't nothing like the real thing, baby,
Ain't nothing like the real thing.
Ain't nothing like the real thing, baby,
Ain't nothing like the real thing.

as (Stevie Wonder)

Stevie Wonder

As around the sun the earth knows she's revolving,
And the rosebuds know to bloom in early May,
Just as hate knows love's the cure,
You can rest your mind assure
That I'll be loving you always.

As now can't reveal the mystery of tomorrow,
But in passing will grow older every day,
Just as all that's born is new,
You know what I say is true,
That I'll be loving you always.

Until the rainbow burns the stars out in the sky,
  Always.
Until the ocean covers every mountain high,
  Always.
Until the dolphin flies and parrots live at sea,
  Always.
Until we dream of life and life becomes a dream.

Did you know that true love asks for nothing?
Her acceptance is the way we pay.
Did you know that life has given love a guarantee
To last through forever and another day?

Just as time knew to move on since the beginning,
And the seasons know exactly when to change,
Just as kindness knows no shame,
Know through all your joy and pain,
That I'll be loving you always.

As today I know I'm living, but tomorrow
Could make me the past, but that I mustn't fear,
For I'll know deep in my mind,
The love of me I've left behind,
'Cause I'll be loving you always.

Until the day is night, and night becomes the day,
  Always.

Until the trees and sea just up and fly away,
Always.
Until the day that eight times eight times eight is four,
Always.
Until the day that is the day that are no more.

Did you know you're loved by somebody?
Until the day the earth starts turning right to left,
Always.
Until the earth just for the sun denies itself,
I'll be loving you forever.
Until dear Mother Nature says her work is through,
Always.
Until the day that you are me and I am you,
Always.
Until the rainbow burns the stars out in the sky,
Always.
Until the ocean covers every mountain high,
Always.

We all know sometimes life's hates and troubles
Can make you wish you were born in another time and space,
But you can bet your life times that and twice its double
That God knew exactly where he wanted you to be placed.
So make sure when you say you're in it but not of it,
You're not helping to make this earth a place sometimes called hell.
Change your words into truths, and then change that truth into love,
And maybe our children's grandchildren
And their great-great grandchildren will tell.

I'll be loving you
Until the rainbow burns the stars out in the sky.
Loving you
Until the ocean covers every mountain high.
Loving you
Until the dolphin flies and parrots live at sea.
Loving you

Until we dream of life and life becomes a dream.
　Be loving you
Until the day is night, and night becomes the day.
　Loving you
Until the trees and seas just up and fly away.
　Loving you
Until the day that eight times eight times eight is four.
　Loving you
Until the day that is the day that are no more.
　Loving you
Until the day the earth starts turning right to left.
　Be loving you
Until the earth just for the sun denies itself.
　Loving you
Until dear Mother Nature says her work is through.
　Loving you
Until the day that you are me, and I am you.
　Now ain't that loving you
Until the rainbow burns the stars out in the sky.
　Ain't that loving you
Until the ocean covers every mountain high.

And I've got to say always
Until the dolphin flies, and parrots live at sea,
　Always.
Until we dream of life, and life becomes a dream,
　Always.
Until the day is night, and night becomes the day,
　Always.
Until the trees and sea just up and fly away,
　Always.
Until the day that eight times eight times eight is four,
　Always.
Until the day that is the day that are no more,
　Always.

Until the day the earth starts turning right to left,
  Always.
Until the earth just for the sun denies itself,
  Always.
Until dear Mother Nature says her work is through,
  Always.
Until the day that you are me, and I am you.

dancing in the street (Marvin Gaye, Ivy Jo Hunter, William "Mickey" Stevenson)

Martha and The Vandellas

Calling out around the world, are you ready for a brand new beat?
Summer's here, and the time is right for dancing in the street.
They're dancing in Chicago
    Dancing in the street,
Down in New Orleans
    Dancing in the street,
In New York City,
    Dancing in the street.

All we need is music, sweet music,
There'll be music everywhere.
There'll be swinging, swaying, and records playing,
    Dancing in the street.

It doesn't matter what you wear, just as long as you are there.
So come on,
Every guy, grab a girl, everywhere around the world.
There'll be dancing, they're dancing in the street.
It's just an invitation, across the nation, a chance for folks to meet.
There'll be laughing, singing, and music swinging,
    Dancing in the street.

Philadelphia PA,
    Dancing in the street
Baltimore and D.C.,
    Dancing in the street
Can't forget the Motor City
    Dancing in the street.

All we need is music, sweet music,
There'll be music everywhere,
There'll be swinging, swaying, and records playing,
    Dancing in the street.

Oh, it doesn't matter what you wear, just as long as you are there.
So come on,
Every guy, grab a girl, everywhere around the world.

They're dancing, they're dancing in the street,
Way down in L.A., every day, they're dancing in the street,
　　Dancing in the street,
Let's form a big strong line, get in time,
　　We're dancing in the street,
Across the ocean blue, me and you,
　　Dancing in the street.

for once in my life (Ron Miller, Orlando Murden)

Stevie Wonder

For once in my life,
I have someone who needs me,
Someone I've needed so long.
For once, unafraid, I can go where life leads me,
Somehow I know I'll be strong.

For once, I can touch what my heart used to dream of,
Long before I knew
Someone warm like you
Would make my dream come true.

For once in my life,
I won't let sorrow hurt me,
Not like it's hurt me before.
For once, I have something I know won't desert me.
I'm not alone anymore.

For once, I can say, this is mine, you can't take it.
As long as I know I have love, I can make it.
For once in my life, I have someone who needs me.

For once in my life,
I won't let sorrow hurt me,
Not like it hurt me before.
For once, I have something I know won't desert me.
I'm not alone anymore.

For once, I can say, this is mine, you can't take it.
Long as I know I have love, I can make it.
For once in my life, I have someone who needs me.

how sweet it is to be loved by you (Edward Holland Jr., Lamont Dozier, Brian Holland)

Marvin Gaye, Junior Walker and The All Stars

How sweet it is to be loved by you,
How sweet it is to be loved by you.

I needed the shelter of someone's arms, and there you were.
I needed someone to understand my ups and downs, and there you were.
With sweet love and devotion,
Deeply touching my emotions.
I want to stop, and thank you, baby,
I want to stop, and thank you, baby.

How sweet it is to be loved by you,
Oh, baby.
How sweet it is to be loved by you.
Yes, it is.

I close my eyes at night,
And wonder what would I be without you in my life.
Everything was just a bore,
All the things I did, seems I'd done them before.
But you brighten up all my days,
With a love so sweet in so many ways.
I want to stop, and thank you, baby,
I want to stop, and thank you, baby.

How sweet it is to be loved by you,
Oh, yes, it is, baby.
How sweet it is to be loved by you.
Yes, it is, baby.

You were better to me than I've been to myself.
For me, there's you and nobody else.
I want to stop, and thank you, baby,
I want to stop, and thank you, baby.

How sweet it is to be loved by you,
Tell the truth, baby.
How sweet it is to be loved by you.
Well, it's like sugar in my soul.
How sweet it is to be loved by you.

if i could build my whole world around you (Johnny Bristol, Vernon Bullock, Harvey Fuqua)

Marvin Gaye and Tammi Terrell

Marvin: If I could build my whole world around you, darlin',
First I'd put heaven by your side.
Pretty flowers would grow wherever you walk, honey,
And over your head would be the bluest sky.
Then I'd take every drop of rain,
And wash all your troubles away.
I'd have the whole world wrapped up in you, darling.
And that would be all right, oh yes, it will.

Tammi: If I could build my whole world around you,
I'd make your eyes the morning sun.
I'd put so much love where there is sorrow.
I'd put joy where there's never been love.
And I'd give my love to you
For you to keep for the rest of your life.
Oh, and happiness would surely be ours,
And that would be all right.

Marvin: Oh, if I could build my whole world around you,
I'd give you the greatest gift any woman could possess.

Tammi: And I'd step into this world you've created,
And give you true love and tenderness.
And there'd be something new with every tomorrow,
To make this world better as days go by.

Marvin: That is if I could build my whole world around you,

Tammi: If I could build my whole world around you,

Both: And that would be all right, oh yeah.

loving you is sweeter than ever (Stevie Wonder, Ivy Jo Hunter)

The Four Tops

I remember yet before we met,
When every night and day I had to live the life of a lonely one.
I remember meeting you,
Discovering love could be so true,
When shared by two instead of only one.

When you said you loved me,
And we could not be parted,
Right then I built my world around you,
I'm so thankful that I found you.

Because loving you has made my life sweeter than ever,
I've never felt like this before.
Loving you has made my life so much sweeter than ever.

Each night I pray we'll never part,
For the love within my heart grows stronger
From day to day.
As best I can, how I try
To reassure you, satisfy,
'Cause I'd be lost if you went away,
Because I really need you,
And I need for you to need me too.
I have built my world around you,
I'm so thankful that I found you.

Because loving you has made my life sweeter than ever,
Loving you has made my life so much sweeter than ever.

Because I really love you,
I'm thankful that you love me, too.
I have built my world around you,
And I'm truly glad I found you.

Because loving you has made my life sweeter than ever,
Loving you, since I've been lovin' you, my life's sweeter than ever,
Since I'm lovin' you, life is sweeter than ever.

the one who really loves you (William "Smokey" Robinson)

Mary Wells

Some other girls are filling your head with jive,
So now you're acting like you don't know that I'm alive.
Love, you better wake up, yeah, before we break up,
And you lose me, little me,
The one who really loves you.

Susie only wants you until the day
That she'll again have her true love who's far,
Far away.
So love, you better wake up,
Yeah, before we break up,
And you lose me, little me,
The one who really loves you.

Jenny only wants you,
'Cause she thinks she has to have everyone.
Minnie only wants you,
'Cause she thinks that hurting me would be fun.
Oh, oh, oh, silly Lilly,
You know she doesn't really
Want you with a love that's true.

In fact, there's no other girl
In this whole wide world
Who can love you like I do.

They get tired of you,
And they're gonna put you down.
Then they ain't gonna want you hangin' around.
So love, you better wake up,
Yeah, before we break up,
And you lose me, little me,
The one who really loves you.

I do,
Really, really love you.

pride and joy (Norman Whitfield, Marvin Gaye, William "Mickey" Stevenson)

Marvin Gaye

You are my pride and joy,
And I just love you, love ya, darlin',
Like a baby boy loves his toy.
You've got kisses sweeter than honey,
And I work seven days a week to give you all my money,
And that's why you are my pride and joy.

And I'm tellin' the world,
You're my pride and joy,
I believe I'm your baby boy,
And I know you're mine,
My pride and joy.
Yeah, baby, yeah, baby.

You, you are my pride and joy,
And a love like mine, yeah, my baby,
Is something nobody can ever destroy.
You pick me up when I'm down,
And when we go out, pretty baby,
You shake up the whole town.
And that's why,
I believe you're my pride and joy.

Yeah, yeah, yeah,
Every day,
In the midnight hour,
I, I'm a baby boy.
Ooo, my pride and joy,
And I love you like a baby loves his toy.
Yeah, yeah, yeah, yeah.

signed, sealed, delivered, i'm yours (Lee Garrett, Lula Mae Hardaway, Stevie Wonder, Syreeta Wright)

Stevie Wonder

Like a fool I went and stayed too long.
Now I'm wonderin' if your love's still strong.
Ooo baby, here I am, signed, sealed, delivered, I'm yours.

Then that time I went and said goodbye,
Now I'm back and not ashamed to cry.
Ooo baby, here I am, signed, sealed, delivered, I'm yours.

Here I am, baby,
Oh, you've got my future in your hand.
Signed, sealed, delivered, I'm yours.

Here I am, baby,
Oh, you've my future in your hand.
Signed, sealed, delivered, I'm yours.

I've done a lot of foolish things
    that I really didn't mean,
Hey, hey, yeah, yeah, didn't I, oh baby.

Seen a lot of things in this old world.
When I touched them they meant nothing, girl.
Ooo baby, here I am, signed, sealed, delivered, I'm yours,
Oh, I'm yours.

Oo-wee babe, you set my soul on fire.
That's why I know you're my heart's only desire.
Ooo baby, here I am, signed, sealed, delivered, I'm yours.

Here I am, baby,
Oh, you've got my future in your hand.
Signed, sealed, delivered, I'm yours.

Here I am, baby,
You've got my future in your hand.
Signed, sealed, delivered, I'm yours.

I've done a lot of foolish things
    that I really didn't mean.
I could be a broken man, but here I—
With your future, got your future, babe,

Here I am, baby
 Signed, sealed, delivered, I'm yours.
Here I am, baby
 Here I am, baby,
Here I am, baby
 Signed, sealed, delivered, I'm yours.
Here I am, baby
 Here I am, baby,
Here I am, baby
 Signed, sealed, delivered, I'm yours.

up the ladder to the roof (Vincent DiMirco, Frank Wilson)

The Supremes

Come with me,
And we shall run across the sky.
And illuminate the night.
Oh, oh, oh, I will try and guide you
To better times and brighter days.
Don't be afraid.

Come on up the ladder to the roof,
Where we can see heaven much better.
Go up the ladder to the roof,
Where we can be closer to heaven.

Stay with me,
And we shall let expression sing.
Can't you hear it ringing?
Oh, memories of yesterday's broken dreams.
Don't you know,
They'll all fade away?
If you'll come.

Come on up the ladder to the roof,
Where we can see heaven much better.
Go up the ladder to the roof,
Where we can be closer to heaven.

We'll laugh, I'll tell you the story of love,
How it is, and the happiness in it, baby.
We'll combine our thoughts, and together we will travel
The roads to the fountain of lovingness.
I will never, never, ever
Leave you, leave you alone to wonder.
As we go up, our love it will grow much stronger, stronger.
Don't you want to go?

Up the ladder to the roof,
Where we can see heaven much better.
Go up the ladder to the roof,
Where we can be closer to heaven.

Up the, up the,
Ooo, up the, up the,
Come on and walk,
Come on and talk,
Come on and sing about love and understanding.
Ooo, up the ladder to the roof,
See heaven.

the way you do the things you do (William "Smokey" Robinson, Bobby Rogers)

The Temptations

You've got a smile so bright,
You know you could've been a candle.
I'm holding you so tight,
You know you could've been a handle.
The way you swept me off my feet,
You know you could've been a broom.
The way you smelled so sweet,
You know you could've been some perfume.

Well, you could've been anything that you wanted to,
And I can tell, the way you do the things you do.

As pretty as you are,
You know you could've been a flower.
If good looks was a minute,
You know that you could be an hour.
The way you stole my heart,
You know you could've been a cool crook.
And, baby, you're so smart,
You know you could've been a schoolbook.

Well, you could've been anything that you wanted to,
And I can tell, the way you do the things you do.

You made my life so rich,
You know you could've been some money.
And, baby, you're so sweet,
You know you could've been some honey.

Well, you could've been anything that you wanted to,
And I can tell, the way you do the things you do.
You really swept me off my feet,
You made my life complete,
You made my life so bright,
You make me feel all right,
You make me feel all right,
You make me feel all right.

you are the sunshine of my life (Stevie Wonder)

Stevie Wonder

You are the sunshine of my life,
That's why I'll always be around.
You are the apple of my eye,
Forever you'll stay in my heart.

I feel like this is the beginning,
Though I've loved you for a million years.
And if I thought our love was ending,
I'd find myself drowning in my own tears.

You are the sunshine of my life,
That's why I'll always stay around.
You are the apple of my eye,
Forever you'll stay in my heart.

You must have known that I was lonely,
Because you came to my rescue,
And I know that this must be heaven.
How could so much love be inside of you?

You are the sunshine of my life,
That's why I'll always stay around.
You are the apple of my eye,
Forever you'll stay in my heart.

you're a wonderful one (Edward Holland Jr., Lamont Dozier, Brian Holland)

Marvin Gaye

You are so wonderful
That being near you is all that I'm living for.
You've shown me more kindness in little ways
Than I've ever known in all my days.
Tell me we'll stay together,
Let me love you forever,
'Cause you're a wonderful one,
You're a wonderful one.

In you there is a rare quality.
Your love, baby, it means the world to me.
For me you're always concerned,
And you ask nothin', baby, in return.
You're really more than I deserve.
From my heart I mean these words,
You're a wonderful one,
You're a wonderful one.

Oh, you're a wonderful one,
Baby, you're a wonderful one.
Sweetheart, you're a wonderful one,
My darlin', you're a wonderful one.
Oh, you're a wonderful one,
Ooo, you're a wonderful one.
Mmm hmm, you're a wonderful one,
Baby, you're a wonderful one.

You're really more than I deserve.
From my heart I mean these words,
You're a wonderful one,
You're a wonderful one.

Sometimes I'm up, sometimes I'm down,
But your love, you're always around.
Words of confidence you speak to me,
Baby, and you place a tender kiss on my cheek.
It makes my burden a little bit lighter,
Makes my life a little bit brighter,

'Cause you're a wonderful one,
You're a wonderful one.

Oh, you're a wonderful one,
Baby, you're a wonderful one.

your precious love (Nickolas Ashford, Valerie Simpson)

Marvin Gaye and Tammi Terrell

Marvin: Every day there's something new,
Honey, to keep me lovin' you.
And with every passin' minute,
Ah baby, so much joy wrapped up in it.

Both: Heaven must have sent you from above,
Heaven must have sent your precious love.

Tammi: And now, I've got a song to sing,
Tellin' the world about the joy you bring.
And you gave me a reason for livin',
And ooo, you taught me, you taught me the meaning of givin'.

Both: Heaven must have sent you from above,
Heaven must have sent your precious love.

Marvin: To find a love like yours is rare these days,
'Cause you've shown me what happiness is in so many ways.

Tammi: I look in the mirror, and I'm glad to see
Laughter in the eyes where tears used to be.

Marvin: What you've given me I could never return,
'Cause there's so much, girl, I've yet to learn.

Tammi: And I wanna show, I wanna show my appreciation,
'Cause when I found you, I found a new inspiration.

Both: Heaven must have sent you from above,
Heaven must have sent your precious love.

when a man loves a woman

bernadette (Edward Holland Jr., Lamont Dozier, Brian Holland)

The Four Tops

Bernadette, people are searching for
The kind of love that we possess.
Some go on searching their whole life through,
And never find the love I've found in you.

And when I speak of you, I see envy in other men's eyes,
And I'm well aware of what's on their minds.
They pretend to be my friend, when all the time
They long to persuade you from my side.
They'd give the world and all they own
For just one moment we have known.

Bernadette, they want you because of the pride that it gives,
But Bernadette, I want you because I need you to live.
But while I live only to hold you,
Some other men, they long to control you.
But how can they control you, Bernadette,
When they cannot control themselves, Bernadette,
From wanting you, needing you.
But, darling, you belong to me.

I'll tell the world you belong to me,
I'll tell the world you're the soul of me,
I'll tell the world you're a part of me.
Bernadette!

In your arms, I find the kind of peace of mind
The world is searching for.
But you, you give me the joy this heart of mine
Has always been longing for.

In you I have what other men long for.
All men need someone to worship and adore.
That's why I treasure you and place you high above,
For the only joy in life is to be loved.
So whatever you do, Bernadette, keep on loving me,
Bernadette, keep on needing me,

Bernadette.

Bernadette!
You're the soul of me
More than a dream,
You're friend of me
And Bernadette,
You mean more to me
Than a woman was ever meant to be.

i can't get next to you (Barrett Strong, Norman Whitfield)

The Temptations

I can turn the grayest sky blue,
I can make it rain whenever I want it to.
I can build a castle from a single grain of sand,
I can make a ship sail on dry land.

But my life is incomplete, and I'm so blue,
'Cause I can't get next to you.

I can't get next to you, babe,
I can't get next to you.
I can't get next to you, babe,
I can't get next to you.

I can fly like a bird in the sky.
Hey, and I can buy anything that money can buy.
I can turn a river into a raging fire.
I can live forever if I so desire.

Unimportant are all these things I can do,
'Cause I can't get next to you.

I can't get next to you, babe, no matter what I do,
I can't get next to you.

I can turn back the hands of time, you better believe I can.
I can make the seasons change just by waving my hand.
I can change anything from old to new.
The thing I want to do the most, I'm unable to do.

Unhappy am I with all the powers I possess,
'Cause, girl, you're the key to my happiness.
And I,
Oh I, I
Can't get next to you.

Girl, you're blowing my mind
'Cause I can't get, next to you.
Can't you see these tears I'm crying?

I can't get, next to you.
Girl, it's you that I need.
I gotta get, next to you.
Can't you see these tears I'm crying?

I can't help myself (Brian Holland, Lamont Dozier, Eddie Holland)

The Four Tops

Sugar pie, honey bunch,
You know that I love you.
I can't help myself,
I love you and nobody else

In and out my life,
You come and you go,
Leaving just your picture behind,
And I've kissed it a thousand times.

When you snap your finger
Or wink your eye,
I come running to you.
I'm tied to your apron string
And there's nothing I can do,

Can't help myself
Can't help myself
Sugar pie, honey bunch,
I'm weaker than a man should be.
I can't help myself, I'm a fool in love you see.

Wanna tell you I don't love you,
Tell you that we're through,
And I've tried,
But every time I see your face,
I get all choked up inside.

When I call your name,
Girl it starts the flame
Burning in my heart,
Tearin' it all apart.
No matter how I try,
My love I cannot hide.

Sugar-pie, honey-bunch,
You know that I'm weak for you.
I can't help myself,
I love you and nobody else.

Sugar-pie, honey-bunch,
I'll do anything you ask me to.
Can't help myself,
I want you and nobody else.

i second that emotion (Al Cleveland, William "Smokey" Robinson)

Smokey Robinson and The Miracles

Maybe you'll wanna give me kisses sweet,
But only for one night with no repeat.
Then maybe you'll go away and never call,
And a taste of honey's worse than none at all.

Oh, little girl, in that case I don't want no part.
I do believe that, that would only break my heart.
Oh, but if you feel like lovin' me,
If you got the notion,
I second that emotion.

Said, if you feel like givin' me
A lifetime of devotion,
I second that emotion.

Maybe you think that love would tie you down,
And you don't have the time to hang around.
Or maybe you think that love was made for fools,
And so it makes you wise to break the rules.

Oh, little girl, in that case I don't want no part.
I do believe that, that would only break my heart.
Oh, but if you feel like lovin' me,
If you got the notion,
I second that emotion.

So, if you feel like givin' me
A lifetime of devotion,
I second that emotion.

In that case I don't want no part.
I do believe that, that would only break my heart.
Oh, but if you feel like lovin' me,
If you got the notion,
I second that emotion.

Said, if you feel like givin' me
A lifetime of devotion,
I second that emotion.
Oh, little girl,
I second that emotion.

i was made to love her (Henry Cosby, Lula Mae Hardaway, Sylvia Moy, Stevie Wonder)

Stevie Wonder

I was born in Little Rock,
Had a childhood sweetheart,
We were always hand in hand.

I wore high-top shoes and shirttails,
Suzy was in pigtails,
I knew I loved her even then.

You know my papa disapproved it,
My mama boohooed it,
But I told them time and time again,
Don't you know I was made to love her?
Build a world all around her.
Yeah! Hey, hey, hey.

She's been my inspiration,
Showed appreciation
For the love I gave her through the years.

Like a sweet magnolia tree,
My love blossomed tenderly,
My life grew sweeter through the years.
I know that my baby loves me,
My baby needs me,
That's why we've made it through the years.

I was made to love her,
Worship, and adore her,
Hey, hey, hey.

All through thick and thin,
Our love just won't end,
'Cause I love my baby, love my baby. Ah!

My baby loves me,
My baby needs me,
And I know I ain't going nowhere.

I was knee-high to a chicken
And that love bug bit me.
I had the fever with each passing year.

Oh, even if the mountain tumbles,
If this whole world crumbles,
By her side I'll still be standing there.

'Cause I was made to love her,
I was made to live for her, yeah, yeah, yeah!

Ah, I was made to love her,
Build my world all around her,
Hey, hey, hey.

Ooo baby, I was made to please her,
You know Stevie ain't gonna leave her, no,
Hey, hey, hey.

let's get it on (Marvin Gaye, Ed Townsend)

Marvin Gaye

I've been really tryin', baby
Tryin' to hold back these feelings for so long.
And if you feel like I feel, baby,
Come on, oh come on,

Let's get it on,
Let's get it on.
Let's love, baby.
Let's get it on,
Let's get it on.

We're all sensitive people
With so much to give, understand me, sugar.
Since we got to be here,
Let's live, I love you.

There's nothin' wrong with me
Lovin' you.
And givin' yourself to me can never be wrong
If the love is true.

Don't you know how sweet and wonderful life can be?
I'm askin' you, baby, to get it on with me.
I ain't gonna worry, I ain't gonna push, won't push you, baby.
So come on, come on, come on, come on, baby,
Stop beatin' around the bush.

Let's get it on,
Let's get it on.
You know what I'm talking about,
Come on, baby, hey, let your love come out.
If you believe in love,
Let's get it on.
Ooo, let's get it on, baby.
Let's get it on.
Please, please get it on.

Come on, come on, come on, come on, come on, darling,
Stop beatin' around the bush.

Ooo, gonna get it on,
Not threatenin' you, baby,
I want to get it on.
You don't have to worry that it's wrong.
If the spirit moves you let me groove you, good.
Let your love come down.

Ooo get it on,
Come on, baby.
Do you know the meaning of being sanctified?
Hey, hey, girl, you give me good feelin',
So good, somethin' like sanctified.

more love (William "Smokey" Robinson)

Smokey Robinson and The Miracles

Let it be soon, don't hesitate,
Make it now, don't wait.
Open your heart and let my love come in.
I want the moment to stop when I can fill your heart

With more love, and more joy
Than age or time could ever destroy.
My love will be so solid
It would take a hundred lifetimes
To live it down, wear it down, tear it down.

This is no fiction, this is no act,
This is real, it's a fact.
I'll always belong only to you,
Each day I'll be living to make sure
I'm giving you

More love and more joy
Than age or time could ever destroy.
My love will be so solid
It would take a hundred lifetimes
To live it down, wear it down, tear it down.

As we grow older, no need to fear,
When you need me, I'll be here.
I'll be beside you every step of the way,
A heart that's truthful and keeping it youthful

With more love, more joy
Than age or time can ever destroy.
My love will be so solid
It would take a hundred lifetimes
To live it down, wear it down, tear it down.

With more love, more joy
Than age or time can ever destroy.

my cherie amour (Henry Cosby, Sylvia Moy, Stevie Wonder)

Stevie Wonder

La la la la la la, la la la la la la.

My cherie amour, lovely as a summer's day,
My cherie amour, distant as the Milky Way,
My cherie amour, pretty little one that I adore,
You're the only girl my heart beats for.
How I wish that you were mine.

In a cafe or sometimes on a crowded street,
I've been near you, but you never noticed me.
My cherie amour, won't you tell me how could you ignore
That behind that little smile I wore
How I wish that you were mine.

La la la la la la, la la la la la la,
La la la la la la, la la la la la la.

Maybe someday you'll see my face among the crowd,
Maybe someday I'll share your little distant cloud.
Oh, cherie amour, pretty little one that I adore,
You're the only girl my heart beats for.
How I wish that you were mine.

La la la la la la, la la la la la la,
La la la la la la, la la la la la la.

my girl (William "Smokey" Robinson, Ronald White)

The Temptations

I've got sunshine
On a cloudy day.
When it's cold outside,
I've got the month of May.
I guess you'd say,
What can make me feel this way?

My girl, my girl, my girl.
Talkin' 'bout my girl,
My girl.

I've got so much honey,
The bees envy me.
I've got a sweeter song
Than the birds in the trees.
Well, I guess you'd say,
What can make me feel this way?

My girl, my girl, my girl.
Talkin' 'bout my girl,
My girl.

I don't need no money,
Fortune, or fame.
I got all the riches, baby,
One man can claim.
Well, I guess you'd say,
What can make me feel this way?

My girl, my girl, my girl.
Talkin' 'bout my girl,
My girl.

I got sunshine on a cloudy day with my girl.
I've even got the month of May with my girl.
Talkin' 'bout, talkin' 'bout, talkin' 'bout my girl.
Ooo, my girl,
That's all I can talk about is, my girl.

my girl has gone (William "Smokey" Robinson, Warren "Pete" Moore, Marvin Tarplin, Ronnie White)

Smokey Robinson and The Miracles

When you were mine,
I loved you so much,
I got a thrill from your every touch.
You went away with somebody else,
Now all I can say to comfort myself is that

My girl is gone,
And said goodbye.
Don't you cry,
Hold your head up high.
Don't give up,
Give love one more try.
'Cause there's a right girl for every guy.

Although your love wasn't right for me,
Good for another it well may be.
Some girls just aren't made for some guys,
And I've got to make myself realize

That my girl is gone,
And said goodbye.
Don't you cry,
Hold your head up high.
Don't give up,
Give love one more try,
There's a right girl for every guy.

Now happiness and all the best
That's all I wish for you, oh baby.
Don't be like me
In misery.
I'm feeling sad and I'm blue,
I said, I'm sad and I'm blue.
Oh yeah, I'm sad and I'm blue,
I said, I'm sad and I'm blue.

Because my girl is gone
And said goodbye.
Don't you cry,
Hold your head up high.
Don't give up,
Give it one more try.
There's a right girl for every guy.

never can say goodbye (Clifton Davis)

The Jackson 5

Never can say goodbye,
No, no, no, no, I
Never can say goodbye.

Even though the pain and heartache
Seem to follow me wherever I go,
Though I try and try to hide my feelings,
They always seem to show.

Then you try to say you're leaving me
And I always have to say no.
Tell me, why is it so?

That I never can say goodbye,
I never can say goodbye.

Every time I think I've had enough
And start heading for the door,
There's a very strange vibration
Piercing me right through the core.
It says, Turn around, you fool, you know you love her more and more.
Tell me, why is it so?

Don't wanna let you go.
I never can say goodbye, girl,
I never can say goodbye,
Oh, I never can say goodbye.
No, no, no, no, no, no, hey

I never can say goodbye,
Never can say goodbye,
No, no, no, no, no, no

I keep thinking that our problems
Soon are all gonna work out.
But there's that same unhappy feeling,
There's that anguish, there's that doubt.
It's the same old dizzy hang-up,
Can't do with you or without.
Tell me, why is it so?
Don't wanna let you go.

I never can say goodbye, girl,
I never can say goodbye.
Ooo, ho, I never can say goodbye, girl,
Ooo, ho, I never can say goodbye, girl.

this old heart of mine (is weak for you) (Edward Holland Jr., Lamont Dozier, Brian Holland, Sylvia Moy)

The Isley Brothers

This old heart of mine been broke a thousand times.
Each time you break away, I feel you're gone to stay.
Lonely nights that come, memories that flow,
Bringing you back again, hurting me more and more.

Maybe it's my mistake to show this love I feel inside,
'Cause each day that passes by,
You've got me never knowin' if I'm comin' or goin', but I

I love you.
   Yes I do, yes I do.
This old heart, darlin', is weak for you.
I love you, yes I do, yes I do.

These old arms of mine miss having you around,
Make these tears inside start falling down.

Always with half a kiss, you remind me of what I miss.
Though I try to control myself,
Like a fool I start grinnin' 'cause my head starts spinnin', 'cause I

I love you.
   Yes I do, yes I do.
This old heart, darlin', is weak for you.
   I love you, yes I do, yes I do.

I try hard to hide my hurt inside.
This old heart of mine always keeps me cryin'.
The way you're treatin' me leaves me incomplete.
You're here for the day, gone for the week.

But if you leave me a hundred times,
A hundred times I'll take you back.
I'm yours whenever you want me
I'm not too proud to shout it, tell the world about it, 'cause I

   I love you.
This old heart is weak for you.
   I love you.

This old heart is weak for you.
    I love you.
This old heart is weak for you.

too busy thinking about my baby (Jamie Bradford, Barrett Strong, Norman Whitfield)

Marvin Gaye

I ain't got time to think about money,
Or what it can buy.
And I ain't got time to sit down and wonder
What makes a birdie fly.

And I don't have the time to think about
What makes a flower grow.
And I've never given a second thought
To where the rivers flow.

Too busy thinking about my baby,
And I ain't got time for nothing else.

I ain't got time to discuss the weather,
How long it's gonna last.
And I ain't got time to do no studies
Once I get out of class.
Tellin' ya, I'm just a fellow,
Said I've got a one-track mind.
And when it comes to thinking about anything but my baby,
I just don't have the time.

Too busy thinking about my baby,
And I ain't got time for nothing else.

The diamonds and pearls in the world
Could never match her worth, no, no.
She's some kind of wonderful, people, tell ya
I got heaven right here on earth.
I'm just a fellow
With a one, one-track mind.
And when it comes to thinkin' about anything but my baby,
I just don't have the time.

Too busy thinking about my baby,
And I ain't got time for nothing else.

Too busy thinking about my baby,
And I ain't got time for nothing else.

you're my everything (Norman Whitfield, Roger Penzabene, Cornelius Grant)
The Temptations

You surely must know magic, girl,
'Cause you changed my life.
It was dull and ordinary,
But you made it sunny and bright.

Now, I was blessed the day I found you,
Gonna build my whole world around you.
You're everything good, girl, and you're all that matters to me.

When my way was dark and troubles were near,
Your love provided the light, so I could see, girl.
Just knowing your love was near when times were bad
Kept the world from closing in on me, girl.

I was blessed the day I found you,
Gonna build my whole world around you.
You're everything good, girl, and you're all that matters to me.

Baby, you're part of every thought I think each day,
Your name is in every phrase my lips say.
Every dream I dream is about you,
Honey, I can't live without you.
Baby, baby, baby.

You're my everything,
You're my everything, yes, you are.
You're my everything.

You're the girl I sing about in every love song I sing.
    You're my everything.
You're my winter, baby, my summer, my fall, and spring.
    You're my everything.

I was blessed the day I found you,
Gonna build my whole world around you.
You're everything good, girl, and you're all that matters to me.
You're my everything, you're my everything.
    Yes, you are, you're my everything.
You're my everything, you're my everything.
    Yes, you are, you're my everything.
You're my everything, you're my everything.

the love of a woman

baby love (Edward Holland Jr., Lamont Dozier, Brian Holland)

The Supremes

Ooo, baby love, my baby love,
I need you, oh how I need you.
But all you do is treat me bad,
Break my heart and leave me sad.
Tell me, what did I do wrong,
To make you stay away so long?

'Cause baby love, my baby love,
Been missing ya, miss kissing ya.
Instead of breaking up,
Let's do some kissing and making up.
Don't throw our love away.
In my arms why don't you stay?
Need ya, need ya,
Baby love, ooo, baby love.

Baby love, my baby love,
Why must we separate, my love?
All of my whole life through,
I never loved no one but you.
Why you do me like you do?
I get this need.

Ooo, ooo, need to hold you
Once again, my love.
Feel your warm embrace, my love.
Don't throw our love away.

Please don't do me this way.
Not happy like I used to be.
Loneliness has got the best of me,
My love, my baby love.

I need you, oh how I need you.
Why you do me like you do,
After I've been true to you,
So deep in love with you?

Baby, baby, ooo, 'til it's hurtin' me,
'Til it's hurtin' me.
Ooo, baby love,
Don't throw our love away,
Don't throw our love away.

come see about me (Edward Holland Jr., Lamont Dozier, Brian Holland)

The Supremes

I've been crying, ooo, ooo
'Cause I'm lonely for you.
Smiles have all turned to tears,
But tears won't wash away the fears
That you're never ever gonna return,
To ease the fire that within me burns.

It keeps me crying, baby, for you,
Keeps me sighin', baby, for you.
So won't you hurry?
Come on, boy, see about me.
  Come see about me.
See about your baby.
  Come see about me.

I've given up my friends just for you.
My friends are gone,
And you have, too.
No peace shall I find,
Until you come back
And be mine.
No matter what you do or say,
I'm gonna love you anyway.

Keep on crying, baby, for you,
I'm gonna keep sighin', baby, for you.
So come on, hurry,
Come on and see about me.
  Come see about me,
See about your baby.
  Come see about me.

Sometimes up,
Sometimes down.
My life's so uncertain
With you not around.

From my arms you may be out of reach,
But my heart says you're here to keep.

Keeps me crying, baby, for you,
Keep on, keep on crying, baby, for you.
So won't you hurry?
Come on, boy, see about me,
    Come see about me,
See about your baby,
    Come see about me.
You know I'm so lonely,
    Come see about me.
I love you only
    Come see about me.
See about your baby
    Come see about me.

don't mess with bill (William "Smokey" Robinson)

The Marvelettes

Don't mess with Bill,
No, no, no, no, don't mess with Bill,
Don't mess with Bill,
Say it one more time,
Don't mess with Bill.

Well, I know he's the guy who put tears in my eyes
A thousand times or more.
Oh, but every time he would apologize,
I loved him more than before.

Hear what I say, girls, keep away,
Don't mess with Bill,
No, no, no, no, don't mess with Bill,
Leave my Billy alone.
Don't mess with Bill,
Get a guy of your own,
Don't mess with Bill.

Now, there's Johnny, there's Joe, and there's Frank and Jim,
Just to name a few.
Now, Bill's got me, and I've got him,
I'm sure there's one for you.

Hear what I say, girls, keep away,
Don't mess with Bill,
No, no, no, no, don't mess with Bill,
He's mine, all mine,
Don't mess with Bill,
I say it one more time,
Don't mess with Bill.

Though I tell myself he wants no one else,
'Cause he keeps coming back to me.
Now I'm in no position to want competition,
I want to be sure as can be.

Hear what I say, girls, keep away,
Don't mess with Bill,
No, no, no, no, don't mess with Bill,
Leave my Billy alone,

Don't mess with Bill,
Get a guy of your own
    Don't mess with Bill,
'Cause he's mine, all mine
    Don't mess with Bill,
I say it one more time.
    Don't mess with Bill,
Yeah, yeah, yeah, yeah,
    Don't mess with Bill,
Yeah, yeah, yeah, yeah.

i hear a symphony (Edward Holland Jr., Lamont Dozier, Brian Holland)

The Supremes

You've given me a true love,
And every day I thank you, love,
For a feeling that's so new,
So inviting, so exciting.

Whenever you're near,
I hear a symphony,
A tender melody
Pulling me closer,
Closer to your arms.

Then suddenly,
Ooo, your lips are touching mine,
A feeling so divine.
'Til I leave the past behind,
I'm lost in a world
Made for you and me.

Whenever you're near,
I hear a symphony,
Played sweet and tenderly,
Every time your lips meet mine now, baby.
Baby, baby,
You bring much joy within.
Don't let this feeling end,
Let it go on and on and on.
Now baby, baby,
Those tears that filled my eyes
I cry not for myself,
But for those who've never felt the joy we felt.

Whenever you're near,
I hear a symphony.
Each time you speak to me,
I hear a tender rhapsody of love now.

Baby, baby,
As you stand holding me,

Whispering how much you care,
A thousand violins fill the air.

Now baby, baby,
Don't let this moment end.
Keep standing close to me,
Ooo, so close to me, baby, baby.
Baby, baby,
I hear a symphony,
A tender melody.

if i were your woman (Gloria Jones, Clay McMurray, Pam Sawyer)

Gladys Knight and the Pips

If I were your woman,
And you were my man,
You'd have no other woman,
You'd be weak as a lamb.
If you had the strength
To walk out that door,
My love would overrule my sense,
And I'd call you back for more.

If I were your woman,
If I were your woman,
And you were my man.

She tears you down, darling,
Says you're nothing at all.
But I'll pick you up, darling,
When she lets you fall.
You're like a diamond,
But she treats you like glass.
Yet you beg her to love you,
But me you don't ask.

If I were your woman,
If I were your woman,
If I were your woman,
Here's what I'd do:
I'd never—no, no—stop loving you,
Yeah.

Life is so crazy,
And love is unkind.
Because she came first,
Will she hang on your mind?
You're a part of me,
And you don't even know it.
I'm what you need,
But I'm too afraid to show it.

If I were your woman,
If I were your woman,
If I were your woman,
Here's what I'd do:
Never—no, no, no—stop loving you.

Oh, yeah
If I were your woman,
Here's what I'd do:
I'd never, never, never stop loving you.
If I were your woman,
You're sweet lovin' woman,
If I were your woman,
I'd be your only woman,
If I were your woman,
You'd need no other woman,
If I were your woman.

my guy (William "Smokey" Robinson)

Mary Wells

Nothing you could say can tear me away from my guy,
Nothing you could do 'cause I'm stuck like glue to my guy.
I'm stickin' to my guy like a stamp to a letter,
Like birds of a feather, we stick together.
I'm tellin' you from the start, I can't be torn apart from my guy.

Nothing you can do could make me untrue to my guy.
Nothing you could buy could make me tell a lie to my guy.
I gave my guy my word of honor to be faithful, and I'm gonna.
You best be believing I won't be deceiving my guy.

As a matter of opinion, I think he's tops.
My opinion is he's the cream of the crop.
As a matter of taste, to be exact,
He's my ideal, as a matter of fact.

No muscle-bound man could take my hand from my guy.
No handsome face could ever take the place of my guy.
He may not be a movie star, but when it comes to being happy,
    we are.
There's not a man today who could take me away from my guy.

No muscle-bound man could take my hand from my guy.
No handsome face could ever take the place of my guy.
He may not be a movie star, but when it comes to being happy,
    we are.
There's not a man today who could take me away from my guy,
There's not a man today who could take me away from my guy,
There's not a man today who could take me away from my guy,
There's not a man today who could take me away from my guy.

please mr. postman (Brian Holland, William Garrett, Georgia Dobbins, Robert Bateman, Freddie Gorman)

The Marvelettes

Wait! Oh yes, wait a minute, Mr. Postman,
Wait! Wait, Mr. Postman.

Please, Mr. Postman, look and see,
Is there a letter in your bag for me?
I been waiting a mighty long time
Since I heard from that boyfriend of mine.

There must be some word today
From my boyfriend so far away.
Please, Mr. Postman, look and see
If there's a letter, a letter for me.
I been standing here waiting, Mr. Postman,
So, so patiently
For just a card or just a letter,
Saying he's returning home to me.

Please, Mr. Postman, look and see,
Is there a letter in your bag for me?
Please, please, Mr. Postman.
'Cause it's been a mighty long time,
Since I heard from that boyfriend of mine.

So many days you passed me by,
You saw the tear standing in my eye.
You wouldn't stop to make me feel better,
By leaving me a card or a letter.

Please, Mr. Postman, look and see,
Is there a letter in your bag for me?
You know it's been so long
Since I heard from that boyfriend of mine.

You better wait a minute, wait a minute,
Oh, you better wait a minute,
Please, please, Mr. Postman,
Please check and see, just one more time for me.

You better wait, wait a minute, wait a minute,
    wait a minute, wait a minute,
Please, Mr. Postman,
Deliver the letter, the sooner the better.
Wait a minute, wait a minute, wait a minute
Please, Mr. Postman.

stop! in the name of love (Edward Holland Jr., Lamont Dozier, Brian Holland)

The Supremes

Stop! In the name of love,
Before you break my heart.

Baby, baby,
I'm aware of where you go
Each time you leave my door.
I watch you walk down the street,
Knowing your other love you'll meet.
But this time before you run to her,
Leaving me alone and hurt,
Think it over: after I've been good to you?
Think it over: after I've been sweet to you?

Stop! In the name of love,
Before you break my heart.
Stop! In the name of love,
Before you break my heart,
Think it over,
Think it over.

I've known of your,
Your secluded nights.
I've even seen her
Maybe once or twice.
But is her sweet expression
Worth more than my love and affection?
But this time, before you leave my arms,
And rush off to her charms,
Think it over: haven't I been good to you?
Think it over: haven't I been sweet to you?

Stop! In the name of love,
Before you break my heart.
Stop! In the name of love,
Before you break my heart,
Think it over,
Think it over.

I've tried so hard, hard to be patient,
Hoping you'll stop this infatuation.
But each time you are together,
I'm so afraid of losing you forever.

Stop! In the name of love,
Before you break my heart.
Baby, think it over,
Stop! In the name of love,
Think it over, baby,
Before you break my heart.
Ooo, think it over, baby . . .

under your spell

baby i need your loving (Edward Holland Jr., Lamont Dozier, Brian Holland)

The Four Tops

Baby, I need your lovin',
Baby, I need your lovin'.

Although you're never near,
Your voice I often hear.
Another day, another night,
I long to hold you tight,
'Cause I'm so lonely.

Baby, I need your lovin',
Got to have all your lovin'.
Baby, I need your lovin',
Got to have all your lovin'.

Some say it's a sign of weakness
For a man to beg.
Then weak I'd rather be,
If it means havin' you to keep,
'Cause lately I've been losin' sleep.

Baby, I need your lovin',
Got to have all your lovin'.
Baby, I need your lovin',
Got to have all your lovin'.

Empty nights,
Echo your name.
Sometimes I wonder
Will I ever be the same?
When you see me smile you know
    And I need you and I want you, baby.
Things have gotten worse.
    And I need you and I love you, baby.
Any smile you might see
    And I need you and I want you, baby.
Has all been rehearsed.
    And I need you and I love you, baby.
Darlin', I can't go on without you.
    And I need you and I want you, baby.

This emptiness won't let me live without you.
   And I need you and I love you, baby.
This loneliness inside me, darlin',
   And I need you and I want you, baby
Makes me feel half alive.
And I need you and I . . .

Baby, I need your lovin',
Got to have all your lovin'.
Baby, I need your lovin',
Got to have all your lovin'.
Baby, I need your lovin',
Got to have all your lovin'.
Baby, I need your lovin',
Got to have all your lovin'.

distant lover (Marvin Gaye, Gwen Gordy Fuqua, Sandra Greene)

Marvin Gaye

Distant lover, lover,
So many miles away.
Heaven knows that I long for you
Every night, every night.
I plan, sometimes I dance
Through the day.

Distant lover,
You should think about me,
And say a prayer for me.
Please, please, baby,
Think about me sometimes,
Think about me here,
Here in misery.

As I reminisce through our joyful summer together,
The promises we made,
All the daily letters.
Then all of the sudden
Everything seemed to explode.
Now I gaze out my window,
Sugar, down a lonesome road.

Distant lover,
Sugar, how can you treat my heart
So mean and cruel?
Didn't you know, sugar?
That every moment that I spent with you,
I treasure the moment like it was a precious jewel.

Please, come back, baby,
Something I wanna say.
When you left,
You took all of me with you.
Do you wanna hear me scream?
Please, please, come back and hold me, girl.

every little bit hurts (Ed Cobb)

Brenda Holloway

Every little bit hurts,
Every little bit hurts.
Every night I cry,
Every night I sigh,
Every night I wonder why
You treat me cold.
Yet you won't let me go.

Every little hurt counts,
Every little hurt counts.
You say you're coming home,
Yet you never phone,
Leave me all alone.
My love is strong for you,
I'd do wrong for you.

I can't take this loneliness you've given me,
I can't go on giving my life away.

Come back to me,
Darling, you'll see
I can give you all the things that you wanted before,
If you will stay with me.

Every little bit hurts,
Every little bit hurts.
To you, I'm a toy
And you're the boy
Who has to say
When I should play.
Yet you hurt me,
Desert me.

Come back to me,
Darling, you'll see
I can give you all the things that you wanted before,
If you will stay with me.

Every little bit hurts,
Every little bit hurts,
Every little bit hurts.

heat wave (Edward Holland Jr., Lamont Dozier, Brian Holland)

Martha and The Vandellas

Whenever I'm with him,
Something inside starts to burning,
And I'm filled with desire.
Could it be a devil in me,
Or is this the way love's supposed to be?

It's like a heat wave
Burnin' in my heart.
I can't keep from cryin',
It's tearin' me apart.

Whenever he calls my name,
Soft, low, sweet, and plain,
Right then, right there,
I feel that burnin' flame.
Has high blood pressure got a hold on me,
Or is this the way love's supposed to be?

It's like a heat wave
Burnin' in my heart.
I can't keep from cryin',
It's tearin' me apart.

Sometimes I stare in space,
Tears all over my face.
I can't explain it,
Don't understand it,
I ain't never felt like this before.
Now that funny feelin' has me amazed,
Don't know what to do,
My head's in a haze.

It's like a heat wave,
Burnin' in my heart,
I can't keep from cryin',
It's tearin' me apart.

Yeah, yeah, yeah, yeah,
Oh, yeah

Yeah, yeah, yeah, yeah,
Oh, yeah.

I feel it burnin',
Right here in my heart . . .

i'll be in trouble (William "Smokey" Robinson)

The Temptations

If you decide to make me blue, I'll be in trouble,
If you decide to be untrue, I'll be in trouble.
'Cause no matter what you do or say,
I know I'm gonna love you anyway.
So if that's what you wanna do, I'll be in trouble.

If you decide one day you want to make a change, love,
You want to leave me here and love a total stranger.
Well, no matter what you do or say,
I know I'm gonna love you anyway.
So if that's what you wanna do, I'll be in danger.

I'll do everything I can to make you stay,
Keep you by my side.
'Cause I love you in such a way,
I'll forget all about my pride.

If you decide you want to go, I'll be in trouble,
I can't prepare myself and so, I'll be in trouble.
So no matter what you do or say,
I know I'm gonna love you anyway.
So I just want you to know I'll be in trouble.

If you decide you want to go, I'll be in trouble,
I can't prepare myself and so, I'll be in trouble.
So no matter what you do or say,
I know I'm gonna love you anyway.
So I just want you to know I'll be in trouble.

love is like an itching in my heart (Edward Holland Jr., Lamont Dozier, Brian Holland)

The Supremes

The love bug done bit me,
Didn't mean for him to get me.
Get up in the morning
And I'm filled with desire.
No, no I can't stop the fire,
Love is a real live wire.
It's a burning sensation
Far beyond imagination.

Love is like an itching in my heart,
Tearing it all apart.
Just an itching in my heart,
And, baby, I can't scratch it.
Keeps me sighing, ooo,
Keeps me yearning.

No, Mama can't help me,
No, Daddy can't help me.
I've been bitten by the love bug
And I need some information
To help me out of this situation.
Now, when you're ill,
You take a pill.
When you're thirsty,
Drink your fill.
What you gonna do, oh yeah,
When love gets a hold,
A hold on you?
Love is like an itching in my heart,
And, baby, I can't scratch it.

Love is a nagging irritation
Causing my heart a complication.
Love is a growing infection
And I don't know the correction.
Got me rockin' and a-reelin'
And I can't shake the feelin'.

Love is like an itching in my heart,
Tearing it all apart.
Just an itching in my heart,
And, baby, I can't scratch it.
Keeps me sighing, ooo,
Keeps me yearning.
Keeps me burning,
Keeps me tossing,
Keeps me turning,
Keeps me yearning.

I've been bitten by the love bug
And I need some information
To help me out of this situation.
Love is a nagging irritation
Causing my heart complication.

I've been bitten by the love bug.

nowhere to run (Edward Holland Jr., Lamont Dozier, Brian Holland)

Martha and The Vandellas

Nowhere to run to, baby,
Nowhere to hide.
Got nowhere to run to, baby,
Nowhere to hide.

It's not love I'm runnin' from,
It's the heartbreak I know will come.
'Cause I know you're no good for me,
But you've become a part of me.
Everywhere I go, your face I see,
Every step I take, you take with me, yeah.

Nowhere to run to, baby,
Nowhere to hide.
Got nowhere to run to, baby,
Nowhere to hide.
I know you're no good for me,
But free of you I'll never be, no.

Each night as I sleep,
Into my heart you creep.
I wake up feelin' sorry I met you,
Hopin' soon that I'll forget you.
When I look in the mirror to comb my hair,
I see your face just a-smilin' there.

Nowhere to run,
Nowhere to hide from you, baby.
Got nowhere to run to, baby,
Nowhere to hide.
I know you're no good for me,
But you've become a part of me.

How can I fight a love
That shouldn't be
When it's so deep, so deep,
Deep inside of me?
My love reaches so high, I can't get over it
It's so wide, I can't get around it, no.

Nowhere to run,
Nowhere to hide from you, baby.
I just can't get away from you, baby,
No matter how I try.
I know you're no good for me,
But free of you I'll never be.

Nowhere to run to, baby,
Nowhere to hide.
Got nowhere to run to, baby,
Nowhere to hide.

standing in the shadows of love (Edward Holland Jr., Lamont Dozier, Brian Holland)

The Four Tops

Standing in the shadows of love,
I'm getting ready for the heartaches to come.
Can't you see me standing in the shadows of love?
I'm getting ready for the heartaches to come.

I wanna run, but there's nowhere to go,
'Cause heartaches will follow me, I know.
Without your love, the love I need,
It's the beginning of the end for me.
'Cause you've taken away all my reasons for living
When you pushed aside all the love I've been giving.
Now, wait a minute,
Didn't I treat you right, now baby, didn't I?
Didn't I do the best I could, now didn't I, didn't I?

So don't you leave me standing in the shadows of love,
I'm getting ready for the heartaches to come.
Don't you see me standing in the shadows of love?
Trying my best to get ready for the heartaches to come.

All alone I'm destined to be, with misery my only company.
It may come today, and it might come tomorrow,
But it's for sure I ain't got nothing but sorrow.
Now, don't your conscience kinda bother you?
How can you watch me cry after all I've done for you?
Now, hold on a minute,
I gave you all the love I had, now didn't I?
When you needed me, I was always there, now wasn't I?

I'm trying not to cry out loud,
You know cryin', it ain't gonna
help me now.

What did I do to cause all this grief?
Now, what did I say to make you want to leave?
Now, wait a minute,
I gave my heart and soul to you, now didn't I?
And didn't I always treat you good, now didn't I?

I'm standing in the shadows of love,
I'm getting ready for the heartaches to come.
Don't you see me standing in the shadows of love?
Trying my best to get ready for the heartaches to come.

until you come back to me (that's what i'm gonna do)
(Stevie Wonder, Clarence Paul, Morris Broadnax)

Stevie Wonder

Though you don't call anymore,
I sit and wait in vain.
I guess I'll rap on your door,
Tap on your windowpane.
I want to tell you, baby,
The changes I've been going through,
Missing you.

Until you come back to me
That's what I'm gonna do.

Why did you have to decide
You had to set me free?
I'm gonna swallow my pride,
And beg you to please see me,
I'm gonna walk by myself
To prove that my love is true,
All for you.

Until you come back to me
That's what I'm gonna do.

Living for you, my dear,
Is like living in a world of constant fear.
Hear my plea, I've got to make you see
That our love is dying.

Although your phone you ignore,
Somehow I must explain.
I'll have to rap on your door,
Tap on your windowpane.
I'm gonna camp by your steps
Until I get through to you.
Change your view.

Until you come back to me
That's what I'm gonna do.
Until you come back to me
That's what I'm gonna do.

you keep me hangin' on (Edward Holland Jr., Lamont Dozier, Brian Holland)

The Supremes

Set me free, why don't you, babe?
Get out my life, why don't you, babe?
'Cause you don't really love me,
You just keep me hangin' on.
You don't really need me,
But you keep me hangin' on.

Why do you keep a-comin' around,
Playing with my heart?
Why don't you get out of my life
And let me make a new start?
Let me get over you
The way you've gotten over me.

Set me free, why don't you, babe?
Let me be, why don't you, babe?
'Cause you don't really love me,
You just keep me hangin' on.
Now, you don't really want me,
You just keep me hangin' on.

You say although we broke up,
You still wanna be just friends.
But how can we still be friends
When seeing you only breaks my heart again?
And there ain't nothing I can do about it.

Set me free, why don't you, babe?
Get out my life, why don't you, babe?
Set me free, why don't you, babe?
Get out my life, why don't you, babe?

You claim you still care for me,
But your heart and soul need to be free.
And now that you've got your freedom,
You wanna still hold on to me.
You don't want me for yourself,
So let me find somebody else, hey.

Why don't you be a man about it
And set me free?
Now, you don't care a thing about me,
You're just using me.
Go on, get out, get out of my life,
And let me sleep at night.
'Cause you don't really love me,
You just keep me hangin' on.

you've really got a hold on me (William "Smokey" Robinson)

Smokey Robinson and the Miracles

I don't like you,
But I love you.
Seems that I'm always
Thinkin' of you.
Though you treat me badly,
I love you madly.

You really got a hold on me,
    You really got a hold on me,
You really got a hold on me,
    You really got a hold on me.

Baby,
I don't want you,
But I need you.
Don't wanna kiss you,
But I need to.
Whoa, you do me wrong now,
My love is strong now.

You really got a hold on me,
    You really got a hold on me,
You really got a hold on me,
    You really got a hold on me.

Baby,
I love you, and all I want you to do is just
Hold me, hold me, hold me, hold me.

Tighter,
Tighter.

I wanna leave you,
Don't wanna stay here,
Don't wanna spend another day here.
Oh-woh-woh, I wanna split now,
I just can't quit now.

You really got a hold on me,
    You really got a hold on me,

You really got a hold on me,
    You really got a hold on me.

Baby,
I love you, and all I want you to do is just
Hold me—please, hold me—squeeze, hold me, hold me.

You really got a hold on me,
I said you really got a hold on me,
You know you really got a hold on me.

love is strange

ain't that peculiar (Warren "Pete" Moore, William "Smokey" Robinson, Robert Rogers, Marvin Tarplin)

Marvin Gaye

You do me wrong, but still I'm crazy about you.
Stay away too long and I can't do without you.
Every chance you get, you seem to hurt me more and more.
But each hurt makes my love stronger than before.
I know flowers grow through rain,
But how can love grow through pain?

Ain't that peculiar,
A peculiarity?
Ain't that peculiar, baby.
Peculiar as can be?

You tell me lies that should be obvious to me.
But I'm so much in love with you, baby, 'til I don't want to see,
That things you do and say are designed to make me blue.
It's a doggone shame my love for you makes all
Your lies seem true.
But if the truth makes love last longer,
Why do lies make my love stronger?

Ain't that peculiar,
Peculiar as can be?
Ain't that peculiar,
A peculiarity?

I cried so much, just like a child that's lost its toy.
Maybe, baby, you think these tears I cry are tears of joy.
A child can cry so much until you do everything they say.
But unlike a child, my tears don't help me to get my way.
I know love can last through years,
But how can love last through tears?

Ain't that peculiar,
A peculiarity?
Ain't it peculiar, honey,
Peculiar as can be?

Said I don't understand it, baby
It's so strange sometimes.
Ain't it peculiar?

choosey beggar (Warren "Pete" Moore, William "Smokey" Robinson)

Smokey Robinson and The Miracles

Beggars can't be choicey, I know,
That's what the people say.
But though my heart is begging for love,
I've turned some love away.

Maybe one was true love,
I'll never know which.
'Cause your love is the only love
To make this beggar rich.

I'm a choosey beggar,
Choosey beggar,
And you're my choice.

People say you can't have your cake
And then eat it, too.
They tell me that I'm making a mistake
Waiting around for you.

I'm begging for love,
But why can't they see
That yours is the only love for me?

I'm a choosey beggar,
Choosey beggar,
And you're my choice.
You're my choice.

If beg you I must, then I'll never give up,
'Cause, your love is the only thing
To fill this beggar's cup.

I'm choosey,
And you're my choice.
When I need someone to hold me,
You're my choice.
When I need arms to enfold me,
You're my choice.
When I need someone beside me,
You're my choice.
If I had you, how happy I'd be.

devil with the blue dress (Fredrick "Shorty" Long, William "Mickey" Stevenson)

Shorty Long

Devil with a blue dress, blue dress, blue dress,
Devil with a blue dress on.
Devil with a blue dress, blue dress, blue dress,
Devil with a blue dress on.

Fee, fee, fi, fi, fo-fo, fum,
Lookin' down the street 'cause here she comes.
Wearin' her wig and shades to match,
She's got high-heel shoes and an alligator hat.
Wearin' her pearls and a diamond ring,
She's got bracelets on her arms, and everything.

She's the devil with a blue dress, blue dress, blue dress,
Devil with a blue dress on.
Devil with a blue dress, blue dress, blue dress,
Devil with a blue dress on.

Perfume's smellin' like Chanel No. 5,
Got to be the finest thing alive.
She walks real cool, catches everybody's eye,
The cats are too nervous to even say Hi.
Not too skinny, she's not too fat,
She's a real humdinger and I like it like that.

She's the devil with a blue dress, blue dress, blue dress,
Devil with a blue dress on.
Devil with a blue dress, blue dress, blue dress,
Devil with a blue dress on.

Fee, fee, fi, fi, fo-fo, fum,
Lookin' down the street 'cause here she comes.
Wearin' her wig and shades to match,
She's got high-heel shoes and an alligator hat.
Wearin' pearls and a diamond ring,
She's got bracelets on her arms, and everything.

She's the devil with a blue dress, blue dress, blue dress,
Devil with a blue dress on.

just my imagination (running away with me) (Norman Whitfield, Barrett Strong)

The Temptations

Each day through my window I watch her as she passes by.
I say to myself, You're such a lucky guy.
To have a girl like her
Is truly a dream come true.
Out of all of the fellows in the world,
She belongs to you.

But it was just my imagination
Running away with me.
It was just my imagination
Running away with me.

Soon we'll be married
And raise a family.
In a cozy little home out in the country
With two children, maybe three.
I tell you, I can visualize it all.
This couldn't be a dream, far too real it all seems.

But it was just my imagination, once again,
Running away with me.
I tell you it was just my imagination
Running away with me.

Every night on my knees I pray,
Dear Lord, hear my plea.
Don't ever let another take her love from me
Or I will surely die.
Ooo, her love is heavenly.
When her arms enfold me,
I hear a tender rhapsody.
But in reality, she doesn't even know me.

Just my imagination, once again,
Running away with me.
Tell you, it was just my imagination
Running away with me.

I never met her, but I can't forget her.
Just my imagination,
Running away with me.

love is here and now you're gone (Edward Holland Jr., Lamont Dozier, Brian Holland)

The Supremes

Love is here,
And oh, my darling, now you're gone.
Love is here,
And oh, my darling, now, now you're gone.

You persuaded me to love you
And I did.
But instead of tenderness,
I found heartache instead.
Into your arms I fell,
So unaware of the loneliness
That was waiting there.

   Look what you've done, look what you've done.
You closed the door to your heart,
And you turned the key, locked your love away from me.

Love is here,
And oh, my darling, now you're gone.

You made me love you,
And oh, my darling, now you're gone.

You said loving you
Would make life beautiful
With each passing day.
But as soon as love
Came into my heart,
You turned and you walked, just walked away.

   Look what you've done, look what you've done.
You stripped me of my dreams,
You gave me faith, then took my hope.
Look at me now.

Look at me,
See what loving you has done to me.
Look at my face,
See how crying has left its trace.

After you made me all your own,
Then you left me all alone.
You made your words sound so sweet,
Knowing that your love I couldn't keep.

    Look what you've done, look what you've done.
My heart cries out for your touch,
But you're not there,
And the lonely cry fades in the air.

Love is here,
And oh, my darling, now you're gone.
Love is here,
And oh, my darling, now you're gone.

You made me love you.
Oh, my darling,
Now you're gone.
You made me love you.
Oh, my darling,
Now you're gone.

truly yours (Ivy Jo Hunter, William "Mickey" Stevenson)

The Spinners, The Temptations

As I read the words written in your letter,
The tears began to rise.
I could read between the lines,
Though you thought it was better not to use the word "goodbye."

And I struggled to hold my pride.
Finally I broke down and cried.

Your letter ended "truly yours,"
But you're no longer truly, truly mine.
Though you signed it "truly yours,"
You're no longer truly, truly mine.
I'm left behind.

Now it's painfully clear that you've been concealing your feelings
    behind lies.
And I feel so foolish to have ever believed you, and to think I even cried.

But the one thing I'll never understand,
How'd you find the nerve to take a pen in your hand and sign your letter
"Truly yours" when you know that you were never truly mine?
How did you sign it "truly yours"
When you know that you were never truly mine?
Just merely lying.

"Truly yours,"
That's what the letter said.
"Truly yours,"
I said that's what the letter read.

Although you're gone and I'm left alone
And we are far apart,
The shell of a man that you discarded behind you
Still loves you with all his heart.

But the one thing I'll never understand,
How'd you find the nerve to take a pen in your hand and sign that letter
"Truly yours" when you know that you were never truly mine?
How did you sign it "truly yours"
When you know that you were never truly mine?

two lovers (William "Smokey" Robinson)
Mary Wells

Well, I've got two lovers, and I ain't ashamed.
Two lovers, and I love them both the same.

Let me tell you 'bout my first lover:
He's sweet and kind and he's mine, all mine.
He treats me good like a lover should,
And makes me love him.
I really, really love him.

Oh, oh, oh, oh,
I love him so,
And I'll do everything I can to let him know.

But I've got two lovers, and I ain't ashamed.
Two lovers, and I love them both the same.

Let me tell you 'bout my other lover:
You know, he treats me bad, makes me sad.
Makes me cry, but still I can't deny
That I love him.
I really, really love him.
Oh, oh, oh, oh,
I love him so,
And I'll do everything I can to let him know.

Darling, well,
Don't you know that I can tell,
Whenever I look at you,
That you think that I'm untrue,
'Cause I say that I love two.
But I really, really do,
'Cause you're a split personality,
And in reality,
Both of them are you.

Well, I've got two lovers, and I ain't ashamed.
Two lovers, and I love them both the same.
Two lovers, and I ain't ashamed.

love lost

come and get these memories (Edward Holland Jr., Lamont Dozier, Brian Holland)

Martha and The Vandellas

Lover, you've gone from me
And left behind so many memories.

Here's your old friendship ring,
I can't wear it no more.
Here's your old love letters,
I can't read them anymore.

Lover, you've gone from me
And left behind so many memories.

Here is that old teddy bear
That you won for me at the state fair.
Here is some old Valentine cards,
Give them to your new sweetheart.

Lover, you've gone from me
And left behind so many memories.

Here's our old favorite record,
I can't stand to hear it anymore.
Here is some old lingering love,
It's in my heart and it's tearing it apart.

Because of these memories,
I never think of anybody but you.
So come on and get 'em,
'Cause I found me somebody new.

Come and get these memories,
    Come and get 'em
    Since you've gone out of my life.
So my mind and my heart can be at ease,
    Come and get 'em
    Since you've gone out of my life.
Give them to your new love,
Give them to your new love,
So come on and get these memories.

fading away (Warren "Pete" Moore, William "Smokey" Robinson, Robert Rogers)
The Temptations

The feeling we used to get whenever our lips met,
Like smoke from a cigarette, it's fading away,
Fading away, fading away.
It hurts me to think about how love where there was no doubt,
Like a cloud when the sun comes out, it's fading away,
Fading away, fading away.

You've changed and it's showing, baby,
You've changed and it's showing.
Tell me, where is your love going?

The plans we were making up, for our never breaking up,
Like dreams when you're waking up, are fading away,
Fading away, fading away.
The good times we shared a lot when you really cared a lot,
Like steam from a coffeepot, it's fading away,
Fading away, fading away.

You've changed and it's showing, baby,
You've changed and it's showing.
Tell me, where is your love going?

Like smoke from a cigarette, or dreams that you soon forget,
Our love from the day we met, it's fading away,
Fading away, fading away.

You've changed and it's showing, baby,
You've changed and it's showing.
Tell me, where is your love going?
Going.

i heard it through the grapevine (Norman Whitfield, Barrett Strong)

Gladys Knight and the Pips, Marvin Gaye

Ooo, I bet you're wonderin' how I knew
'Bout your plans to make me blue
With some other guy you knew before.
Between the two of us guys,
You know I love you more.
It took me by surprise, I must say,
When I found out yesterday.
Don't you know that

I heard it through the grapevine,
Not much longer would you be mine.
Oh, I heard it through the grapevine,
Oh, and I'm just about to lose my mind,
Honey, honey, yeah.

I know a man ain't supposed to cry,
But these tears I can't hold inside.
Losin' you would end my life, you see,
'Cause you mean that much to me.
You could have told me yourself
That you love someone else.
Instead

I heard it through the grapevine,
Not much longer would you be mine.
Oh, I heard it through the grapevine,
And I'm just about to lose my mind,
Honey, honey, yeah.

People say believe half of what you see,
Some or none of what you hear.
But I can't help bein' confused.
If it's true, please tell me, dear.
Do you plan to let me go
For the other guy you loved before?
Don't you know

I heard it through the grapevine,
Not much longer would you be mine.

Baby, I heard it through the grapevine,
Ooo, I'm just about to lose my mind.

Honey, honey, I know
That you're letting me go.
Said I heard it through the grapevine,
Ooo, heard it through the grapevine.

(i know) i'm losing you (Cornelius Grant, Edward Holland Jr., Norman Whitfield)

The Temptations

Your love is fading,
I can feel your love fading.
Girl, it's fading away from me.
'Cause your touch, your touch has grown cold,
As if someone else controls your very soul.
I've fooled myself long as I can,
I can feel the presence
Of another man.

It's there when you speak my name,
It's just not the same.
Ooo, baby, I'm losing you.
It's in the air,
It's everywhere.
Ooo, baby, I'm losing you.

When I look into your eyes,
A reflection of a face I see.
I'm hurt, downhearted, and worried, girl;
'Cause that face doesn't belong to me.

It's all over your face,
Someone's taken my place.
Ooo, baby, I'm losing you.
You try hard to hide,
The emptiness inside.
Ooo, I can tell, I'm losing you.

I don't wanna lose you . . .

I can tell when we kiss
From the tenderness I miss,
Ooo, little girl, I'm losing you.
I can feel it in my bones,
Any day you'll be gone.
Ooo, baby, I'm losing you.

Oh, my dear, what happened to the love we shared?
Ooo, baby, I'm losing you.

never dreamed you'd leave in summer (Stevie Wonder, Syreeta Wright)

Stevie Wonder

I never dreamed you'd leave in summer,
I thought you would go, then come back home.
I thought the cold would leave by summer,
But my quiet nights will be spent alone.

You said there would be warm love in springtime,
That is when you started to be cold.
I never dreamed you'd leave in summer,
But now I find myself all alone.

You said then you'd be the life in autumn,
Said you'd be the one to see the way.
I never dreamed you'd leave in summer,
But now I find my love has gone away.

Why didn't you stay?

i want you back (The Corporation: Berry Gordy Jr., Alphonso Mizell, Freddie Perren, Deke Richards)

The Jackson 5

When I had you to myself I didn't want you around,
Those pretty faces always made you stand out in a crowd.
But someone picked you from the bunch, one glance was all it took,
Now it's much too late for me to take a second look.

Oh baby, give me one more chance to show you that I love you.
Won't you please let me back in your heart?
Oh darling, I was blind to let you go, let you go, baby,
But now since I see you in his arms, I want you back.

Oh, I do now,
I want you back.
Ooo, ooo, baby,
I want you back.
Yeah, yeah, yeah, yeah
I want you back.
Nah, nah, nah, nah.

Trying to live without your love is one long sleepless night,
Let me show you, girl, that I know wrong from right.
Every street you walk on, I leave tearstains on the ground,
Following the girl I didn't even want around.

Oh baby, all I need is one more chance to show you that I love you.
Won't you please let me back in your heart?
Oh darling, I was blind to let you go, let you go, baby,
But now since I see you in his arms,
All I want, all I need, all I want, all I need.

Oh, just one more chance to show you that I love you,
Baby, baby, baby, baby, baby, baby,
I want you back.
Forget what happened then,
Let me live again.

Oh baby, I was blind to let you go,
But now since I see you in his arms, I want you back.

Spare me of this cost,
Give back what I lost.

Oh baby, I need one more chance,
I tell you that I love you!
Baby, baby, baby, I want you back.

i wish it would rain (Barrett Strong, Norman Whitfield, Roger Penzabene)

The Temptations

Sunshine, blue skies, please go away,
My girl has found another and gone away.
With her went my future, my life is filled with gloom,
So day after day, I stay locked up in my room.

I know to you, it might sound strange,
But I wish it would rain.
   Oh, how I wish that it would rain.
Oh yeah, yeah, yeah, yeah.

'Cause so badly
I wanna go outside
   Such a lovely day.
But everyone knows that a man ain't supposed to cry,
Listen, I got to cry, 'cause crying,
Eases the pain, ah yeah.

People, this hurt I feel inside
Words could never explain.
I just wish it would rain
   Oh, how I wish that it would rain.
Oh let it rain, rain, rain, rain.
   Oh, how I wish that it would rain,
Ooo baby.

Let it rain, let it rain,
Oh yeah, let it rain.

Day in, day out, my tear-stained face
Pressed against my windowpane.
My eyes search the skies desperately for rain
'Cause raindrops will hide my teardrops, and no one will ever know
That I'm crying, crying, crying, crying
When I go outside.

To the world outside my tears I refuse to explain,
I wish it would rain,
   Oh, how I wish that it would rain,
Ooo baby. Let it rain.
I need rain to disguise
   the tears I cry.

it's the same old song (Edward Holland Jr., Lamont Dozier, Brian Holland)

The Four Tops

You're sweet as a honeybee,
But like a honeybee stings,
You've gone and left my heart in pain.
All you left is our favorite song,
The one we danced to all night long.
It used to bring sweet memories
Of a tender love that used to be.

Now it's the same old song,
But with a different meaning
Since you been gone.
It's the same old song,
But with a different meaning
Since you been gone.

A sentimental fool am I
To hear an old love song and wanna cry.
But the melody keeps haunting me,
Reminding me how in love we used to be.
Keep hearing the part that used to touch our hearts,
Saying together forever,
Breaking up never.

It's the same old song,
But with a different meaning
Since you been gone.
It's the same old song,
But with a different meaning
Since you been gone.

Precious memories keep a-lingering on,
Every time I hear our favorite song.
Now you're gone,
Left this emptiness.
I only reminisce
The happiness we spent.
We used to dance to the music,
Make romance to the music.

Now it's the same old song,
But with a different meaning
Since you been gone.
It's the same old song,
But with a different meaning
Since you been gone.

Oh I,
Can't bear to hear it.
It's the same old song,
But with a different meaning
Since you been gone.

lately (Stevie Wonder)

Stevie Wonder

Lately I have had the strangest feeling
With no vivid reason here to find.
Yet the thought of losing you has been hanging
　'round my mind.

Far more frequently you're wearing perfume
With, you say, no special place to go.
But when I ask, will you be coming back soon?
You don't know, never know.

Well, I'm a man of many wishes,
Hope my premonition misses.
But what I really feel my eyes won't let me hide,
'Cause they always start to cry,
'Cause this time could mean goodbye.

Lately I've been staring in the mirror,
Very slowly picking me apart.
Trying to tell myself I have no reason
　with your heart.

Just the other night while you were sleeping,
I vaguely heard you whisper someone's name.
But when I ask you of the thoughts you're keeping,
You just say nothing's changed.

Well, I'm a man of many wishes,
I hope my premonition misses.
But what I really feel my eyes won't let me hide,
'Cause they always start to cry,
'Cause this time could mean goodbye, goodbye.

Oh, I'm a man of many wishes,
I hope my premonition misses.
But what I really feel my eyes won't let me hide,
'Cause they always start to cry,
'Cause this time could mean goodbye.

my world is empty without you (Edward Holland Jr., Lamont Dozier, Brian Holland)

The Supremes

My world is empty without you, babe,
My world is empty without you, babe.

And as I go my way alone,
I find it hard for me to carry on.
I need your strength,
I need your tender touch,
I need the love, my dear,
I miss so much.

My world is empty without you, babe,
My world is empty without you, babe.

From this old world
I try to hide my face.
But from this loneliness
There's no hiding place.
Inside this cold and empty house I dwell,
In darkness with memories
I know so well.

I need love now
More then before.
I can hardly
Carry on anymore.

My world is empty without you, babe,
Without you, babe,
My world is empty without you, babe.

My mind and soul
Have felt like this
Since love between us
No more exists.
And each time that darkness falls
It finds me alone
With these four walls.

My world is empty without you, babe,
Without you, babe,
My world is empty without you, babe,
Without you, babe,
Without you, babe.

ooo baby baby (William "Smokey" Robinson, Warren Moore)

Smokey Robinson and The Miracles

I did you wrong.
My heart went out to play,
But in the game I lost you.
What a price to pay.
I'm crying,
Ooo baby baby,
Ooo baby baby.

Mistakes, I know I've made a few,
But I'm only human.
You've made mistakes, too.
I'm crying,
Ooo baby baby,
Ooo baby baby.

I'm just about at
The end of my rope,
But I can't stop trying,
I can't give up hope.
'Cause I feel
One day I'll hold you near,
Whisper I still love you.
Until that day is here
I'm crying.
Ooo baby baby,
Ooo baby baby,
Ooo baby baby,
Ooo baby baby,
Ooo-ooo-ooo-ooo.

reflections (Edward Holland Jr., Lamont Dozier, Brian Holland)

Diana Ross and the Supremes

Through the mirror of my mind,
Time after time,
I see reflections of you and me.

Reflections of
The way life used to be.
Reflections of
The love you took from me.

Oh, I'm all alone now,
No love to shield me,
Trapped in a world
That's a distorted reality.

Happiness you took from me,
And left me alone
With only memories.

Through the mirror of my mind,
Through these tears that I'm crying,
Reflects a hurt I can't control.
'Cause although you're gone,
I keep holding on
To the happy times,
Ooo, when you were mine.

As I peer through the window
Of lost time,
Looking over my yesterdays
And all the love I gave all in vain,
    All the love,
All the love
That I've wasted,
    All the tears,
All the tears
That I've tasted,
All in vain.

Through the hollow of my tears,
I see a dream that's lost,
From the hurt
That you have caused.

Everywhere I turn,
Seems like everything I see
Reflects the love that used to be.

In you I put
All my faith and trust.
Right before my eyes,
My world has turned to dust.

After all of the nights
I sat alone and wept,
Just a handful of promises
Are all that's left of loving you.

Reflections of
The way life used to be.
Reflections of
The love you took from me.

In you I put
All my faith and trust.
Right before my eyes
My world has turned to dust.

rocket love (Stevie Wonder)

Stevie Wonder

I longed for you since I was born,
A woman sensitive and warm
And that you were.

With pride and strength no one would test,
But yet have feminine finesse
And so much more.

You took me riding in your rocket, gave me a star,
But at a half a mile from heaven you dropped me back
    down to this cold, cold world.
Took me riding in your rocket, gave me a star,
But at a half a mile from heaven you dropped me back
    down to this cold, cold world.

A female Shakespeare of your time,
With looks to blow Picasso's mind,
You were the best.

Your body moved with grace and song,
Like symphonies by Bach or Brahms.
Nevertheless,

You took me riding in your rocket, gave me a star,
But at a half a mile from heaven you dropped me back
    down to this cold, cold world.
You took me riding in your rocket, gave me a star,
But at a half a mile from heaven you dropped me back
    down to this cold, cold world.

The passion burning in your heart
Would make hell's fire seem like a spark.
Where did it go?

Just why then you would overnight
Turn love to stone as cold as ice,
I'll never know.

But you took me riding in your rocket, gave me a star,
But at a half a mile from heaven you dropped me back
    down to this cold, cold world.

Baby, you took me riding in your rocket, gave me a star,
But at a half a mile from heaven you dropped me back
   down to this cold, cold world.

Cold, too cold, you took me riding in your rocket, gave me a star,
But at a half a mile from heaven you dropped me back
   down to this cold, cold world.
Oh, oh, oh, took me riding in your rocket, gave me a star,
But at a half a mile from heaven you dropped me back
   down to this cold, cold world.

7 rooms of gloom (Edward Holland Jr., Lamont Dozier, Brian Holland)

The Four Tops

I see a house, a house of stone,
A lonely house, 'cause now you're gone.
Seven rooms, that's all it is,
Seven rooms of gloom.
I live with emptiness, without your tenderness.

You took the dream I had for us,
Turned my dreams into dust.
I watch a phone that never rings,
I watch your door that never brings,
Brings you back into my life, turns this darkness into light.
I'm all alone in this house, turn this house into a home.

I need your touch to comfort me,
Your tender, tender arms that once held me.
Without your love, your love inside,
This house is just a place to run and hide.
Seven rooms, that's all it is,
Seven rooms of gloom.
Rooms of emptiness, without your tenderness.

Don't make me live from day to day,
Watching a clock that ticks away.
Another day, another way, another reason for me to say,
I need you here, here with me,
I need you, darling, desperately.
I'm all alone, all alone in this house that's not a home.

I miss your love I once had known,
I miss your kiss that was my very, very own.
Empty silence surrounding me, lonely walls they stare at me.
Seven rooms, that's all it is,
Rooms of gloom.
I live with emptiness, without your tenderness.

All the windows are painted black,
And wait right here until you get back.
I'll keep waiting, waiting,
'Til your face again I see.

shake me, wake me (when it's over) (Edward Holland Jr., Lamont Dozier, Brian Holland)

The Four Tops

All through this long and sleepless night,
I hear my neighbors talking,
    She don't love him.
Saying that out of my life into another's arms
You'll soon be walking.

Somebody, shake me, wake me when it's over.
Somebody, tell me that I'm dreaming
And wake me when it's over.

They say our love ain't what it used to be,
And everyone knows but me.
I close my ears not wanting to hear,
But the words are loud and clear.

Through these walls so thin,
I hear my neighbors when they say,
    She don't love him, she don't love him.
They say my heart's in danger,
'Cause you're leaving me
For the love of a stranger.

Somebody, shake me, come on and wake me, somebody,
    when it's over.
Somebody, tell me that I'm dreaming
And wake me when it's over.

Girl, you're what my heart desires,
My whole world you've inspired.
I can't bear to be losing you,
'Cause I've loved you my whole life through.

Restlessly,
I pace the floor,
Listening to my neighbors criticize.
What a fool I am not to realize
You don't want me by your side.
As the tears stream down my face,

I can't believe I've been replaced.
If I've ever, ever, dreamed before,
Somebody tell me I'm dreaming now.

And then shake me, wake me, somebody, when it's over.
Somebody, tell me, tell me that I'm dreaming
And wake me when it's over.

since i lost my baby (William "Smokey" Robinson, Warren Moore)

The Temptations

The sun is shining, there's plenty of light,
A new day is dawning, sunny and bright.
But after I've been crying all night,
The sun is cold and the new day seems old

Since I lost my baby,
Oh, since I lost my baby.

The birds are singing and the children are playing,
There's plenty of work and the bosses are paying.
Not a sad word should a young heart be saying,
But fun is a bore and with money I'm poor

Since I lost my baby,
Oh, since I lost my baby.

Next time I'll be kinder,
Won't you please help me find her?
Someone just remind her
Of this love she left behind her.
'Til I find her I'll be trying to,
Every day I'm more inclined to
Find her,
Inclined to
Find her,
Inclined to find my baby,
Been looking everywhere,
Baby, I really, really care.

Oh, determination is fading fast,
Inspiration is a thing of the past.
Can't see how my hope's gonna last.
Good things are bad and what's happy is sad

Since I lost my baby,
Oh, since I lost my baby.

I feel so bad,
I feel so sad.
Everything is wrong,

This heart is hard to carry on.
I'm lost as can be,
What's gonna happen to me?

take me in your arms (rock me) (Edward Holland Jr., Lamont Dozier, Brian Holland)

The Isley Brothers and Kim Weston

Take me in your arms,
Hold me for a little while.

I know you're leavin' me behind,
I'm seein' you, darlin', for the very last time.
Show a little tenderness before you go,
Please let me feel your embrace once more.

Take me in your arms, rock me, rock me a little while,
Hold me, darling, rock me, rock me a little while.

We all must feel heartache sometimes,
Right now, right now I'm feelin' mine.
I've tried my best to be strong, but I'm not able,
I'm like a helpless child left in a cradle.
Let me know the joy before I grieve,
Just once more, darling, before you leave.

Take me in your arms and rock me, rock me a little while,
Hold me, darling, rock me, rock me a little while.

I'm losing you and my happiness,
My life is over, I must confess.
I'll never, never see your smiling face no more,
I'll never, never hear your knock on my door.
Before you leave me, leave me behind,
Let me feel happy just one more time.

Take me in your arms, rock me, rock me a little while,
Hold me, darling, rock me, rock me a little while.

I said I wouldn't beg,
I said I wouldn't plead.
Here I am, baby, begging you, please,
Baby, please,
Baby, please.
Take me in your arms, rock me, rock me a little while,
Hold me, darling, take me in your arms.

the tears of a clown (Henry Cosby, William "Smokey" Robinson, Stevie Wonder)

Smokey Robinson and The Miracles

Now if there's a smile on my face,
It's only there tryin' to fool the public.
But when it comes down to foolin' you,
Now, honey, that's quite a different subject.

But don't let my glad expression
Give you the wrong impression.
Really I'm sad,
Ah, sadder than sad.
You're gone and I'm hurtin' so bad,
Like a clown I pretend to be glad.

Now there's some sad things known to man,
But ain't too much sadder than
The tears of a clown
When there's no one around.

Now if I appear to be carefree,
It's only to camouflage my sadness.
In order to shield my pride, I try
To cover this hurt with a show of gladness.

But don't let my show convince you
That I've been happy since you
Decided to go.
Oh, I need you so.
I'm hurt and I want you to know,
But for others I put on a show.

Oh, there's some sad things known to man,
But ain't too much sadder than
The tears of a clown
When there's no one around, oh yeah.

Just like Pagliacci did,
I try to keep my sadness hid.
Smiling in the public eye,
But in my lonely room I cry
The tears of a clown
When there's no one around.

Now if there's a smile on my face,
Don't let my glad expression
Give you the wrong impression.
Don't let this smile I wear
Make you think that I don't care.
Really I'm sad,
Hurtin' so bad.

the tracks of my tears (Warren "Pete" Moore, William "Smokey" Robinson, Marvin Tarplin)

Smokey Robinson and The Miracles

People say I'm the life of the party
'Cause I tell a joke or two.
Although I might be laughin' loud and hearty,
Deep inside I'm blue.

So take a good look at my face.
You'll see my smile looks out of place.
If you look closer, it's easy to trace
The tracks of my tears.

I need you,
Need you.

Since you left me if you see me with another girl,
Seemin' like I'm havin' fun,
Although she may be cute,
She's just a substitute,
Because you're the permanent one.

So take a good look at my face.
You see my smile looks out of place.
Yeah, look a little bit closer, it's easy to trace,
Oh, the tracks of my tears.

Oh-ho-ho-ho, I need you,
Need you.

Hey, hey, yeah,
Outside, I'm masquerading,
Inside, my hope is fading.
I'm just a clown, ooo yeah, since you put me down
My smile is my makeup
I wear since my breakup with you.

Baby, take a good look at my face, uh-huh.
You'll see my smile looks out of place.
Yeah, just look closer, it's easy to trace,
Oh, the tracks of my tears.

Baby, baby, baby, baby,
Take a good look at my face.
Ooo yeah, you see my smile looks out of place.
Look a little bit closer, it's easy to trace,
Yeah, the tracks of my tears.

what becomes of the brokenhearted (James Dean, Paul Riser, William Weatherspoon)

Jimmy Ruffin

As I walk this land of broken dreams,
I have visions of many things.
But happiness is just an illusion
Filled with sadness and confusion.

What becomes of the brokenhearted
Who had love that's now departed?
I know I've got to find
Some kind of peace of mind.
Help me, please.

The roots of love grow all around,
But for me, they come a-tumbling down.
Every day, heartaches grow a little stronger,
I can't stand this pain much longer.

I walk in shadows, searching for light,
Cold and alone, no comfort in sight.
Hoping and praying for someone who'll care,
Always moving and going nowhere.

What becomes of the brokenhearted
Who had love that's now departed?
I know I've got to find
Some kind of peace of mind
Help me, please.

I'm searching, though I don't succeed,
For someone's love there's a growing need.
All is lost, there's no place for beginning,
All that's left is an unhappy ending.

Now, what becomes of the brokenhearted
Who had love that's now departed?
I know I've got to find
Some kind of peace of mind.
I'll be searching everywhere
Just to find someone to care.

I'll be looking every day,
I know I'm gonna find a way.
Nothing's gonna stop me now,
I'll find a way somehow.
I'll be searching everywhere.

where did our love go (Edward Holland Jr., Lamont Dozier, Brian Holland)
The Supremes

Baby, baby,
Baby, don't leave me,
Ooo, please don't leave me
All by myself.

I've got this burning, burning,
Yearning feelin' inside me,
Ooo, deep inside me,
And it hurts so bad.

You came into my heart
So tenderly,
With a burning love
That stings like a bee.

Now that I surrender
So helplessly,
You now wanna leave,
Ooo, you wanna leave me.

Ooo, baby, baby,
Where did our love go?
Ooo, don't you want me,
Don't you want me no more?

Baby, baby,
Where did our love go?
And all of your promises
Of a love forevermore?

I've got this burning, burning,
Yearning feelin' inside me,
Ooo, deep inside me,
And it hurts so bad.

Before you won my heart,
You were a perfect guy.
But now that you got me,
You wanna leave me behind,
Baby, baby, ooo baby, baby.

Baby, baby, don't leave me,
Ooo, please don't leave me,
All by myself.

Ooo, baby, baby,
Where did our love go?

who's lovin' you (William "Smokey" Robinson)

Smokey Robinson and The Miracles, The Jackson 5

When I had you here,
I treated you bad and wrong, my dear.
And, girl, since you been away,
Don't you know I sit around
With my head hanging down,
And I wonder who is lovin' you.

I should have never, never, never made you cry
And since, girl, since you've been gone,
I sit around
With my head hanging down,
And I wonder who is lovin' you.

Life without love is oh so lonely,
I don't think I'm gonna make it.
All my life, all my love, belongs to you only,
Come on home, girl,
Come on and take it because

All I can do, all I can do
Since you been gone is cry.
And don't you ever wonder,
And worry your pretty little head
'Bout what I do.
Don't you know I sit around
With my head hanging down,
And wonder who is lovin' you.

yester-me, yester-you, yesterday (Bryan Wells, Ron Miller)

Stevie Wonder

What happened to the world we knew?
When we would dream and scheme
And while the time away,
Yester-me, yester-you, yesterday.
Where did it go, that yester glow?
When we could feel
The wheel of life turn our way.
Yester-me, yester-you, yesterday.

I had a dream, so did you,
Life was warm and love was true.
Two kids who followed all the rules
Yester-fools, and now,
Now it seems those yester-dreams
Were just a cruel
And foolish game we used to play,
Yester-me, yester-you, yesterday.

When I recall what we had
I feel lost, I feel sad
With nothing but the memory of yester-love, and now,
Now it seems those yester-dreams
Were just a cruel
And foolish game we had to play.
Yester-me, yester-you, yesterday,
Yester-me, yester-you, yesterday,
Sing with me,
Yester-me, yester-you, yesterday.
One more time . . .

higher love

love's in need of love today (Stevie Wonder)

Stevie Wonder

Good morn or evening, friends,
Here's your friendly announcer.
I have serious news to pass on to everybody.
What I'm about to say
Could mean the world's disaster,
Could change your joy and laughter to tears and pain.

It's that
Love's in need of love today.
Don't delay,
Send yours in right away.
Hate's goin' round,
Breaking many hearts.
Stop it, please,
Before it's gone too far.

The force of evil plans
To make you its possession.
And it will, if we let it,
Destroy everybody.
We all must take
Precautionary measures.
If love and peace you treasure,
Then you'll hear me when I say,

Oh, that
Love's in need of love today.
Don't delay,
Send yours in right away.
Hate's goin' round,
Breaking many hearts.
Stop it, please,
Before it's gone too far.

what's going on (Marvin Gaye, Alfred Cleveland, Renaldo Benson)

Marvin Gaye

Mother, Mother, there's too many of you crying,
Brother, Brother, Brother, there's far too many of you dying.
You know we've got to find a way,
To bring some lovin' here today, hey.

Father, Father, we don't need to escalate,
You see, war is not the answer, for only love can conquer hate.
You know we've got to find a way,
To bring some lovin' here today, oh.

Picket lines
   Sister and picket signs
   Sister,
Don't punish me
   Sister with brutality
   Sister,
Talk to me
   Sister
So we can see
   Sister,
Oh, what's goin' on, what's goin' on, what's goin' on, what's goin' on?

Mother, Mother, everybody thinks we're wrong.
Oh, but who are they to judge us,
Simply 'cause our hair is long?
Oh, you know we've got to find a way,
To bring some understanding here today, oh, oh, oh.

Picket lines
   Brother and picket signs
   Brother,
Don't punish me
   Brother with brutality
   Brother.
Come on, talk to me
   Brother

So you can see
  Brother,
Now what's goin' on, what's goin' on, yeah, what's goin' on, what's
  goin' on?
Tell me what's goin' on—what's goin' on?
I'll tell you what's goin' on—what's goin' on.

acknowledgments

The making of *Motown in Love* could itself be an epic tome. This book would not be possible without the patience, resolve, generosity, and support of a dedicated team. To Bob Gottlieb, a sage who snaps to attention at the sound of a great idea. To Margaret Jordan, a writer's writer. Without your guidance and wisdom, this book would not have been possible. I am grateful. To Gary Fears, whose knowledge of Motown and unwavering support were invaluable. And, let it be said, every book should have a Jodi Fodor. To Smokey Robinson, Barrett Strong, Clay McMurray, and Morris Broadnax for sharing the back story. To Khira Jordan, a writer on the horizon. And Kamau Jordan, for always being there. There are many others who have earned my thanks, including Kim Heron, Clarence Avant, Suzanne de Passe, Altie Karper, Diana Tejerina, Janice Goldklang, Daniel Frank, Teddy Harris, Victoria Pearson, Alena Graedon, Jovanka Ciares, Bill Shannon, Nancy Weshkoff, David Altschul, Patty Romanowski, Iris Weinstein, Archie Ferguson, Barbara Martin, Kenya Howard, Michael Johnson, Jonathan Hyams, and Helen Ashford. And to Lula Mae Hardaway, Viola Liuzzo, and Kenneth Cockrel. And a thanks to the staff at Random House, Pantheon, and The Detroit Public Library's Azalia Hackley Collection of Blacks in the Performing Arts.

a note on the lyrics

The lyrics as presented were compiled from a combination of official lyric sheets generated by Motown copyists for copyright registration and from repeated listening to the original recordings. The presentation required the exercise of editorial judgment in a number of areas. In some instances, the lyrics as written diverged from the vocal version. In others, there were variations between different recorded versions of the same song. The presentation mirrors the creative process by which the compositions became the records we know. Consistent with the African American tradition of Call and Response, the lyricists typically anticipated and even left space for the collaborative element of vocalists contributing ad-libs or responsive phrases. The original lyric sheets reveal that some of the background or responsive parts were, in fact, part of the original lyric. In other cases, they were not. In some instances, a lyric line is split between the lead and background vocalists. We've included the ad-lib or background vocal where the line is so integral to the song that, if removed, it would be missed. *How Sweet It Is to Be Loved by You* seems to lose something without Marvin Gaye's "it's like sugar in my soul." Finally, the use of colloquial pronunciations was a conscious device by the writers and vocalists to convey a particular attitude. These choices are reflected in the presentation. While some of the lyrics are exacting in their observance of Standard English, others shorten or reshape words for effect. Ultimately, the goal has been to reflect the intent of the writers and to make the reading of lyrics an enjoyable experience.

lyric permissions acknowledgments

photo permissions acknowledgments

a note about the author

Herb Jordan is a legal scholar, composer,
and commentator on American culture,
and music producer. He taught at the University of
Michigan Law School, where he received the L. Hart
Wright outstanding faculty member award. He is the
recipient of a Thomas M. Cooley Distinguished
Brief Award for scholarly legal writing. Jordan
composed for Count Basie and produced a number
of award-winning albums including the Grammy-
nominated *American Song*. He tutors young writers
in the Los Angeles Public Schools.

a note on the type

The text of this book was set in Electra, a typeface
designed by W. A. Dwiggins (1880–1956). This face
cannot be classified as either modern or old style.
It is not based on any historical model, nor does it
echo any particular period or style. It avoids the
extreme contrasts between thick and thin elements
that mark most modern faces, and it attempts to
give a feeling of fluidity, power, and speed.

Composed by
North Market Street Graphics,
Lancaster, Pennsylvania

Printed and Bound by
R. R. Donnelley & Sons,
Harrisonburg, Virginia

Designed by
Iris Weinstein